Jean Heaver

COUNTRY PEOPLE

An Endangered Species

British Library Cataloguing in Publication Data

**A catalogue record for this book is available
from the British Library**

ISBN 0 9512619 8 3

First published 2000, by
SMH BOOKS
Pear Tree Cottage, Watersfield, Pulborough,
West Sussex, RH20 1NG
Tel. 01798 831260

Typeset by Michael Walsh
MusicPrint, Chichester

Printed and bound in Great Britain by
RPM Reprographics, Chichester

COUNTRY PEOPLE

An Endangered Species

An Anthology

compiled by

TONY HODGSON

for my mother,

Rosemary Hodgson

who (during her lifetime)

inspired me to love the country

and the people who have shaped it.

CONTENTS

Chapter 5 CREATURES

Chapter 6 CHANGE

Chapter 7 SPIRIT

ACKNOWLEDGEMENTS

We acknowledge, with thanks, the granting of permissions for copyright material to be reproduced in this book by the following publishers, agents and persons:

Miss Olivia Swinnerton (for extracts from ENGLISH MAIDEN by Frank Swinnerton); Mr Fred Archer (for extracts from his WHEN VILLAGE BELLS WERE SILENT and HAWTHORN HEDGE COUNTY); Mr Roger Mason (for extracts from his GRANNY'S VILLAGE); Random House UK Ltd (for an extract from THE SEA FOR BREAKFAST by Lilian Beckwith, Hutchinson, 1962), SILVER WEDDING by Maeve Binchy, Century Hutchinson, 1988, LIGHT A PENNY CANDLE by Maeve Binchy, Hodder & Stoughton, 1983; TUDOR FAMILY PORTRAITS by Barbara Winchester, Jonathan Cape, 1955, and IN SEARCH OF ENGLAND by H V Morton, Methuen, 1932); Mr Peter Razzell (for extracts from BROTHER TO THE OX by Fred Kitchen, Caliban, 1981); The Society of Authors (for extracts from GONE RUSTIC by Cecil Roberts, Hodder & Stoughton, 1934, MEN OF THE EARTH, by H J Massingham, Chapman and Hall, 1943, WHERE MAN BELONGS by H J Massingham, Collins, 1946, and A SHROPSHIRE LAD by A E Housman (Jonathan Cape, 1945); Mrs Elizabeth Chatwin (for an extract from ON THE BLACK HILL, by Bruce Chatwin, Pan Books, 1983); Penguin UK (for extracts from VILLAGE SCHOOL by Miss Read, Michael Joseph, 1955, RING OF BRIGHT WATER by Gavin Maxwell, Penguin Books, 1974, RED SKY AT NIGHT by John Barrington, Michael Joseph, 1984, GULL ON THE ROOF by Derek Tangye, 1986, THE GAMEKEEPER by Barry Hines, Michael Joseph, 1975, and THE GO-BETWEEN by L P Hartley, Hamish Hamilton, 1953); John Murray (Publishers) Ltd (for extracts from YEOMAN FARMER'S SON by Harold Cramp and the poem *Lines Written to Martyn Skinner,* from COLLECTED POEMS by John Betjeman, John Murray, 1982); Mr Owen Chadwick (for an extract from VICTORIAN MINIATURE, Hodder and Stoughton, 1960); Mrs Pamela McCormick (for an extract from FARMER'S GLORY, by A G Street, Penguin, 1971); Lady Susan Chitty (for an extract from her THE BEAST AND THE MONK, Hodder & Stoughton, 1975, and CHARLES KINGSLEY'S LANDSCAPE, David & Charles, 1976); Little Brown (for extracts from I KNOW MY PLACE by Edward Short, MacDonald, 1983) and FEN WOMEN by Mary Chamberlain (Virago, 1975); Miss Anthea Bell (for extracts from SILVER LEY by Adrian Bell, Oxford University Press, 1931, and THE CHERRY TREE by Adrian Bell, Oxford University Press, 1932); Mrs C Roma Fletcher (for an extract from THE PARKERS AT SALTRAM by Ronald Fletcher, BBC Publications, 1970); the Rev'd Robin Pagan (for an extract from Reform Magazine, November, 1988); Mr Peter Moore (for an

i

extract from SON OF A RECTORY by Aubrey Moore, Alan Sutton, 1982); Josephine Howarth (for an extract from her THE COUNTRY HABIT, Methuen, 1987); The Regents of the University of California (for an extract from SAINT FRANCIS: NATURE MYSTIC, University of California Press, 1973); International Thomson Publishing Services Ltd (for an extract from THE CHANGING YEAR by Proteus, Unwin, 1985); Frederick Warne (for an extract from THE JOURNAL OF BEATRIX POTTER 1881-1897 (Frederick Warne, 1966); Cambridge University Press (for an extract from JOSEPH ASHBY OF TYSOE by M K Ashby, Merlin Press, 1974), David & Charles (for an extract from THE COUNTRY PARSON by Simon Goodenough, David & Charles, 1983); Elizabeth West (for an extract from her GARDEN IN THE HILLS, Corgi, 1985), Mrs Jane Moore (for an extract from THE COMMON STREAM by Rowland Parker, Collins, 1975); A P Watt Ltd, on behalf of Michael Holroyd (for extracts from THE WORM FORGIVES THE PLOUGH by John Stewart Collis, Moray, 1936); Robert Hale (for extracts from NEW COUNTRY TALK by J H B Peel); Peak District National Park Authority (for 'Village Voice', an article in Peak Palk News, Spring, 1983); James Clarke & Co (for an extract from SCOTCH BROTH by Anne Hepple, Lutterworth Press, 1940); Curtis Brown Ltd on behalf of the Estate of Jan Struther (for an extract from MRS MINIVER by Jan Struther, Chatto & Windus, 1939; The Rev'd Jim Wilkinson (for an extract from his MIRACLE VALLEY, Marshall, Morgan & Scott, 1984); Macmillan US (for an extract from FATHER, author unknown, Macmillan, London, 1931); Messrs Charles Russell on behalf of the Estate of Laurie Lee (for extracts from I CAN'T STAY LONG by Laurie Lee, Penguin, 1977 and CIDER WITH ROSIE by Laurie Lee, Hogarth Press, 1959); A M Heath & Co Ltd on behalf of the Estate of the late Noel Streatfeild (for an extract from A VICARAGE FAMILY, Penguin, 1968); Faber & Faber (for an extract from COUNTRY WORLD by Alison Uttley, Faber & Faber, 1986, and the poem 'The Horses' by Edwin Muir, from COLLECTED POEMS by Edwin Muir, Oxford University Press, 1965); Mr Ronald Blythe (for an extract from AKENFIELD: PORTRAIT OF AN ENGLISH VILLAGE, Allen Lane, 1969); Carcanet Press (for a poem 'March Hares' by Andrew Young, from ANDREW YOUNG Selected Poems, Carcanet Press, 1998, and an extract from the Chapter 'A Remembered Harvest', from UNDER STORM'S WING by Helen Thomas, Carcanet Press, 1988); Laurence Pollinger and the Estate of Frieda Lawrence Ravagli (for an extract from THE VIRGIN AND THE GYPSY by D H Lawrence, Penguin, 1982); Laurence Pollinger and the Estate of H E Bates, (for an extract from MY UNCLE SILAS by H E Bates, Penguin, 1958 and an extract from THE ENGLISH COUNTRYSIDE by H E Bates, Batsford, 1943); Laurence Pollinger (for an extract frrom CONSTABLE

ROUND THE VILLAGE by Nicholas Rhea, Robert Hale, 1981); Laurence Pollinger and the Estate of Ralph Whitlock (for extracts from A FAMILY AND A VILLAGE by Ralph Whitlock, John Baker, 1969), and LARK RETURNING by Elisabeth McNeill, Headline, 1989), Peters, Fraser & Dunlop (for extracts from COME RAIN, COME SHINE by John Moore, Collins, 1956, THE BLUE FIELD by John Moore, Collins, 1948, MY SMALL COUNTRY LIVING by Jeanine McMullen, Unwin, 1984, and CORPORAL TUNE by L A G Strong, Gollancz, 1934); Ashgrove Press (for extracts from THE FARMER, THE PLOUGH AND THE DEVIL by Arthur Hollins, Ashgrove Press, 1984); The Countryman (for articles which appeared in that magazine, by John McNeillie, Summer, 1939, Jeannie Pomeroy, and John Manners, Spring, 1976); Shepheard-Walwyn (Publishers) Ltd. (for an extract from BETWEEN HIGH WALLS by Grace Foakes, Shepheard-Walwyn, 1972), and David Higham Associates (for extracts from A HORSEMAN RIDING BY by R F Delderfield, Hodder & Stoughton, 1981, THE LION AND THE UNICORN by Arthur Bryant, Collins, 1969, TWO QUIET LIVES by David Cecil, Constable, 1948, A PORTRAIT OF JANE AUSTEN by David Cecil, Penguin, 1983, THE NINE TAILORS by Dorothy L Sayers, Eyre & Spottiswoode, 1934, IT SHOULDN'T HAPPEN TO A VET by James Herriot, Michael Joseph, 1972, VETS MIGHT FLY by James Herriot, Michael Joseph, 1976, A COUNTRY GIRL AT HEART by Margaret Cole, Brechusett, 1985, THE COUNTRYMAN'S BEDSIDE BOOK by Denys Watkins-Pitchford ('B B'), Eyre & Spottiswoode, 1942, and THE VILLAGE by Marghanita Laski, Cresset Press, 1983).

Special thanks must go to The Society of Authors, and Dr David Sutton and colleagues, of W A T C H (Writers and their Copyright Holders), based at the Library of the University of Reading who (as with our book AN EXALTATION OF SKYLARKS, compiled by Stewart Beer) have been of immeasurable assistance.

For permission to use photographs, we acknowledge the Hulton Getty Picture Collection, West Sussex Record Office, Mr Brian Walker, Mr Richard Phillips, for the photograph of his father, and Mrs Robin Ravilious and the Beaford Archive for photographs by James Ravilious. We would like to thank especially Mr David Swinscoe and Mr Tony Blore for allowing us to use so many pictures from SWINSCOE, BLORE AND THE BASSETTS (Churnett Valley Books, 1998).

Every effort has been made to contact copyright-holders, so that due acknowledgements might be made. Where, inadvertently, we have failed in this endeavour, we apologise and invite any concerned to contact us, if they so wish.

Sandra Saer

for SMH BOOKS

INTRODUCTION

Country people in Britain are an endangered species. This anthology illustrates something of what would be lost if forces infiltrating from cities and suburbs were to make them disappear altogether. It is not an exercise in nostalgia, nor in recrimination. It is an attempt to chronicle the lives of people who have lived and worked in the rural areas of Britain through the last few centuries. Like all human beings they have their faults as well as their saving graces. However, they have had something unique to contribute to the national character, even though recently that contribution may not seem to have carried much weight. It appears that we live in an age when urban society is trying to forget its peasant roots – but it never will.

In many areas births, deaths and marriages are still occasions for communal as well as private celebrations. In small rural communities, the birth of a child may make all the difference between their survival or their withering away. Where a community has a school, every baby born there is a vital asset to ensure its future, too.

In the few closely-knit communities that remain, a marriage may mean the joining together of two whole tribes, with far-reaching ramifications in the surrounding district, or it may even be a marriage within the tribe.

Funerals are liable to bring together scores of people from the vicinity, for whom the death seems like the severing of important links in the chain of human existence.

Growing up in the country was, until recently, quite distinctive. Most children had close contact with the land, and even times at school were governed by the requirement for children to help with farm work. All schooling took place within a mile or two of home and was often integrated into the life of the community.

This has changed, and most country children are now prepared for participation in a modern state which does not necessarily see the rural dimension as important.

Marriage in the country was often a working relationship, based both on division of labour and the sharing of common tasks. Romance certainly could feature in the beginning and there were, no doubt, some excellent partnerships, but whatever the degree of happiness or misery that existed beneath the surface, the comparative stability of rural life contributed to the stability of marriage and family life.

Country people either died young or, if they survived into old age, generally had an honoured place in the society which they had probably served all their lives. Old age and death were a natural part of the cycle repeated every year in the seasons and every few years in the creatures by which country people have been surrounded.

As elsewhere, there have always been extremes of wealth and poverty in rural areas. In earlier centuries, the poverty was usually mitigated by the possession of a small plot of land. With the onset of enclosures, however, landlessness became the curse of the rural poor, a process which reached its climax at the beginning of the nineteenth century.

The eighteenth century saw the creation of vast country mansions, often built with wealth from the lucrative slave trade. These tended to distance their owners from the people who lived in the immediate vicinity. Farmers, who were not major landowners, craftsmen and tradesmen, for example, were not generally accepted as equals by the gentry but saw themselves as several cuts above the labourer. Professional people, such as clergy and doctors and their wives, could themselves come from among the ranks of the aristocracy and, therefore, mix easily with the people 'at the top', while others of lower birth mixed more naturally elsewhere.

Until the First World War, and the disillusionment and disruption that flowed from it, attendance at Church in most rural areas was normal. Much has been said about the iniquity of squires insisting on their retainers attending Services under their eye but, despite all that, there was a great deal of real Christian devotion among country dwellers.

Over the centuries, country people have tolerated a strange succession of changes, usually imposed upon them from outside. In the sixteenth century, they had to learn to abandon the Latin Mass, which they and their forebears had used from time immemorial. In the seventeenth century, they were forced to ricochet between earnest puritan divine, saintly scholar and high church royalist. By the eighteenth century, they were being ministered-to by a poverty stricken curate who was very much like themselves, or by a hunting, drinking parson, more like their squire.

The nineteenth century offered them the additional choice of leaving the parish church for the chapel down the road. The slumber in their parish church might well be broken by a reforming Anglo-Catholic or Evangelical, determined to turn everything upside down, one way or another.

Despite all these changes and chances, country people have continued to see their church building with all its wonderful symbols as a vital focus for their community – often, today, the only focus left.

Many earlier occupations have now disappeared. Few rural craftsmen survived the impact of the Industrial Revolution. Little farm work is now done without the use of a machine.

But there is still continuity: those blacksmiths who managed to weather the lean years, when horses ceased to be used on the land, are now often in great demand from the new users of horses; there are still country men and women who take endless care over their gardens, and some of the old crafts have been revived, and the renewed interest in organic food production has led to the return of more traditional methods of cultivation in some places.

One of the greatest changes in the countryside has been the virtual disappearance of working animals. As recently as the 1950s, all but the most progressive farms still used horses to do some of their work. Now the horse has become a leisure animal – in the process, revolutionising human-animal relationships.

Almost the only animal still used at all as a fellow-worker is the sheepdog. For this reason, sheepdog trials continue to feature largely in rural life, especially in hill country. However, even now, one of the distinctive features of rural communities is that they contain within themselves animal species as well as the human.

Traditionally, country people's attitudes to animal compatriots have ranged from the callous to the loving, but there is a general absence of sentimentality. Animals have been a source of food, and of sport. They have been used for work, protected when useful, and exterminated when seen as pests. But to many they have also been a wonderful source of joy, with glimpses of the truth, recently re-discovered, that animals have as much right to their territory as humans have.

Looking back over country life during the past five centuries, since the break-up of the medieval pattern, can we discern a Golden Age from which there has been a decline, or a steady improvement in the quality of life? One thing cannot be denied: over the last two and a half centuries, there has been a constant leeching of country people from the land, either into the urban areas of this country, or overseas. This process has been aided by a mixture of neglect, greed, ambition, modernisation, and deliberate Government policy.

It is more difficult to defend the arbitrary and violent clearing away of the Highland crofters than a steady stream of of redundancies among farm workers, brought on by the introduction of ever bigger and more sophisticated machines. Yet the effect, in both cases, has been the same.

In the last two or three decades, those leaving have been replaced by people moving to the country from towns and suburbs. Unwittingly, this phenomenon has put additional pressure on the few remaining country people, since the next generation, with housing prices having risen -— and rising – to meet demand, can now seldom afford to stay in their old communities, even if they should wish to. And the 'incomers' have also brought with them non-rural values which have contributed to the acceleration of change.

So what are the rural values which are in danger of being lost for ever?

It is commonly thought that country people are somewhat unwelcoming and suspicious towards outsiders; if they have been so at times, it may not have been without good reason. But towards those who are found trustworthy and wanting to belong, there can be a warmth of welcome and a generosity of heart which goes beyond merely commercial considerations. In very small rural communities, there has been an all-embracing sense of belonging into which all could enter, unless for some reason they have chosen not to, or were ostracised.

Such a group used to be able to protect at least some of its weaker members: the 'village idiot' had a definite place in a society with more important criteria than intellectual ability. There was no need to boast of achievements, since people's strong points as well as their failings were known. 'Characters', too, had their place, as they posed no serious threat to the stability of that society.

For those living in the country who have been above the poverty line, life has often been a source of deep peace and contentment.

And whether they have thought of themselves as religious or not, God has existed for them in the budding of trees in springtime, the singing of birds, the curve of hill and valley and rustling of streams, as well as in the rites and rituals of the Church, non-established or established, and in the breaking-through of the miraculous.

A O L Hodgson

Checkley

2000

Chapter 1

STAGES

BIRTH

The sun set, and Reuben had given up even the attempt to work. He wandered on Boarzell till the outline of its crest was lost in the black pit of night. Then a new anxiety began to fret him. Possibly all was going well since everybody said so, but – suppose the child was a girl! Up till now he had scarcely thought of such a thing, he had made sure that his child would be a boy, someone to help him in his struggle and to reap the fruits of it after he was gone. But suppose, after all, it should be a girl! Quite probably it would be – why should he think it would not? The sweat stood on Reuben's forehead.

Then suddenly he saw something white moving in the darkness. It was coming towards him. It was his mother's apron.

He ran to meet her, for his legs tottered so that he could not walk. He could not frame his question, but she answered it:

"All's well ... it's a boy."

Sheila Kaye-Smith
(1887 – 1956)

Sussex Gorse

She was born in the summer, and was a late fall in my life, and lay purple and dented like a little bruised plum, as though she'd been lightly-trodden in the grass and forgotten.

Then the nurse lifted her up and she came suddenly alive, her bent legs kicking crabwise, and her first living gesture was a thin wringing of the hands accompanied by a far-out Hebridean lament.

This moment of meeting seemed to be a birthtime for both of us; her first and my second life. Nothing, I knew, would be the same again, and I think I was reasonably shaken.

Laurie Lee
(1914 – 1997)

I CAN'T STAY LONG

Miss Judith Whelpdale was born in October, at night, in the middle of a gale which disturbed the tiles and chimney-pots of Shaffle. She was a small baby; but when smacked she gave so loud a scream that Dr. Winter and the nurse both laughed, and Sally, weakened by labour, hurt herself by shaking with inward merriment.

'Nothing the matter with those lungs,' said Dr. Winter, addressing the patient.

Sally, still stupid, prayed: May there never be! The doctor's words made her think at once of Florrie, and, sorrowing because her mother had missed the proud joy of this moment, she wept. Dr. Winter bent over her.

'All well,' he said, in a low voice. 'She's a beauty. A happiness to you for many years.'

'She,' thought Sally. 'Like me!' But whatever profound reflection might have followed the news was lost; for she fell asleep.

The doctor and nurse whispered together, their heads a few inches from Judith's blanket-protected pink body, while the eyes in her bland, bald head were close shut.

'You think a genius, nurse?', teased Dr. Winter.

'Go by the mouth and chin.'

'They're her mother's. That's confirmation, d'you see? I brought her into the world, don't forget. Heigho! I'm getting old. What age would you give me, nurse?'

The nurse, dark and beautiful, with the smooth cheeks of a nun, answered in amused respect.

'Well, you're over thirty.'

'Ha! I'm nearly fifty; yes, I'm forty-eight.'

They saw the door stealthily open in defiance of medical controls; and both assumed busy, obstetrical frowns. It was well that they did so, for Victor's face, pale with spiritual travail, and heavy-eyed from a night-long vigil, was the first to intrude. It was then displaced by Victor's whole presence; while another, calmer, and even more beautiful face immediately followed. Victor's concern was for his sleeping wife; Hermione's all for the still bundle in the nurse's arms. Both showed alarm, which was chased away by broad smiles when nurse and doctor nodded satisfactory assurances. Hermione, after one look at Judith, grimaced deprecatingly.

'Pudgy little wretch!' she exclaimed. 'Ugly as sin!'

'Nurse says she'll be a genius,' laughed Dr. Winter.

'I go by the mouth and chin,' repeated the nurse, at which Hermione ejaculated:

'Good God! We don't want any more instability!'

'Oh, but the instability of genius is an exploded notion!' cried the doctor. 'Remember Shakespeare, Bach, Isaac Newton and Sally...!'

They laughed in whispers. Victor, who had not troubled to examine his daughter, scowled at such levity.

'Sh!' he hissed. 'don't wake her—'

'Which? They're both "hers"...' Dr. Winter was jubilant. 'You're surrounded by women. The bachelor's dream; but it soon turns into a nightmare!'

At that, Victor gave his attention unwillingly to Judith, whom he surveyed at first with repulsion and then, progressively, with tolerance, pleasure and enthusiasm.

'A genius, you say? Of course!' The release of his natural high spirits carried him to ecstatic vision. 'Isn't that what we undertook to supply?' He took Judith in his arms, and marched about the room upon tiptoe. 'Oh, she's a feather! A queen!'

'He's just remembered who begat her!' cried Dr. Winter.

Frank Swinnerton
(1884 – 1982)

English Maiden ·

I did manage to earn quite a lot of money that summer, and it came about in this way. School holidays were arranged to suit the farmers; at least, Whitsuntide and harvest holidays. If Whitsun came early we had one week then and five weeks in harvest. If Whitsun fell when the turnips were ready for singling we got two or three weeks' holiday according to the convenience of the farmers, with either three or four weeks for harvest. No matter which way it came, most of the lads, and lassies, too, spent their holidays singling turnips. And what a back-aching job it was! But I enjoyed it after the first few days. Along with two other lads I worked a fortnight at a shilling a day during the Whitsun holiday, and listened, I have to confess, with relish, to the coarse jokes of the men hoeing turnips. I did even better in the summer, putting five weeks at turnip singling without missing a day, staying a week longer than the school holiday.

Fred Kitchen
(b.1891)

BROTHER TO THE OX

Although, at ten, I seemed to have learnt a prodigious amount in my five years at school, what I had acquired there, apart from my love of nature, was really nothing more than a few useful skills with words and numbers, a collection of facts which were not blindingly relevant to my life in Warcop and a memorised anthology of theological prose – most of which I did not understand. The other ninety-five per cent of my education up to that time had come from the village community which had always passed on to each new generation – and indeed felt obliged to do so – its knowledge, its crafts, its hobbies and its lore. This was community education in its original sense, and how rich and varied it was! The establishment of the village schools in the nineteenth century by the two national societies and, after 1870, by the new School Boards, scarcely dented the old communal sense of responsibility for seeing that the next generation was brought up as useful members of the community.

Edward Short

I KNOW MY PLACE

He was a nice boy, lively and affectionate, who liked his Uncle Benjamin's fruitcake and loved to ride with Uncle Lewis on the tractor.

In the school holidays, his mother sent him to stay for weeks on end; they came to dread, as much as he did, the first day of term.

Perched on the tractor mudguard, he would watch the plough-share bite into the stubble, and the herring-gulls shrieking and swooping over the fresh-turned furrow. He saw lambs being born, potatoes harvested, a cow calving and, one morning, there was a foal in the field.

The twins said all this, one day, would be his.

They fussed over him like a little prince, waited on him at table, learned never to serve cheese or beetroot and, in the attic, found a humming-top that whined like a contented bee. Wilfully retracing the steps of their own childhood, they even thought of taking him to the seaside.

Some nights, his eyelids heavy with sleep, he'd rest his head on his hands and yawn, 'Please, please will you carry me?' So they carried him upstairs to their old bedroom, and undressed him; and put on his pyjamas, and tiptoed out with the night-light burning.

In a patch of garden, he planted lettuces, radishes and carrots, and a row of sweet-peas. He liked listening to the zinging sound of seeds in their packets, but saw no point in sowing biennials.

'Two years,' he'd moan. 'That's far too long to wait!'

With a bucket slung over his arm, he went off scouring the hedges for anything that took his fancy – toads, snails, furry caterpillars – and once he came home with a shrew. When his tadpoles grew into baby frogs, he built a frog-castle, on a rock in the middle of an old stone trough.

Bruce Chatwin
(1940 – 1989)

ON THE BLACK HILL

Bundled in overcoats, for the Spring was late that year, the three girls were ordered by Miss Herbert into the garden, or into what at St. Peter's Vicarage passed for a garden. At the far end of the lawn on the top of a bank there was a privet hedge beyond which, across a path, lay St. Peter's Church. This end of the garden belonged to the children for it was divided from the lawn by a wooden trellis, behind which in a row lay their gardens. When as mere babies they had first come to live in the vicarage the children's voices as they gardened had made passing parishioners think of the twittering of sparrows, but now they were older and had learnt it was ill-manners to raise your voice.

Isobel, crouched over her garden, looked despondently at a daffodil, still only leaves with no sign of a bud in spite of care which had included covering the shoot with sawdust during a hard frost.

"I wish I'd bought snowdrops and crocuses like I did last year. I like to see the beginnings of Spring early."

Louise, who had been raking a corner of her bed, looked up. Her voice took a pathetic note.

"If I had all the pocket-money you get now you are thirteen I'd have every sort of bulb and every sort of plant. I'd have so many there wouldn't be a space between plants."

Victoria, the middle girl, who was twelve, had not been attending to her garden. With her arms folded she had been scowling up at the church spire. She took her eyes away from the spire.

"Don't listen to her, Isobel, you know she's going to make you buy her a plant." Then, turning to Louise: "If you want extra seeds or something go looking all sugar and spice at the man in the plant shop. He'll give you something extra. He always does."

Isobel was an artist. She had drawn and painted before she could write the alphabet. Now she looked with amusement at Victoria, always the fighter and the rebel. "You needn't bother, Vicky, you know perfectly well I wouldn't give anything away." She looked down at her garden. "I'm not really keen on gardening. If it wasn't supposed to be good for you I would give it up."

Noel Streatfeild
(1895 – 1986)

A VICARAGE FAMILY

Suddenly a thick-set girl detached herself from a group and shot an odd question at Susan.

'Have you a bathroom in your house?' she asked in a loud voice which carried across the room. She smiled a little sidelong smile and looked to see if the others were listening. 'Have you a bathroom? You're a train-girl, aren't you? You're a scholarship girl?'

Susan confessed they had no bathroom. Heads nodded, skirts flounced, and the dark girl turned away.

'She says she lives in a house without a bathroom.'

It was a damning fact, no bathroom could ever be built at Windystone, or the troughs might dry up. All the springs on the hillside would be dislocated, and the cattle would have nothing in their troughs. Drinking water for cattle and horses and man came before bathrooms. Susan was disconcerted. She hoped they wouldn't pursue the question of bathrooms. Now if this Eva had asked if there was a water closet, Susan could have boasted that there was and the seat was made from a church pew and the tassel was thick red velvet. As for the view from the window, it was superb. But other girls had no bathrooms and there was an embarrassed air as they looked at one another. Even as they stood undecided the cookery mistress came across and interrupted.

'When will you be returning to Manchester, Eva?' she asked quietly. 'You are only here for this term, are you not? I expect you find our ways different from yours. Many of us in the country have no bathrooms, but we have other consolations.'

Eva blushed and retreated among the girls, but Miss Dobbin's grey eyes twinkled. She was a friendly woman, with no awe-inspiring cap and gown, but a white apron and starched cuffs.

She asked Susan where she lived and smiled when she heard. She knew the villages round Windystone and she too came by train.

Alison Uttley
(1884 – 1976)

COUNTRY WORLD

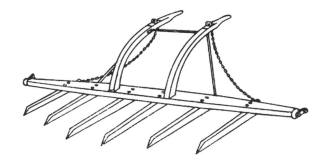

There are a couple of hundred village boys taking the courses in agriculture and on the whole I'd say that Christianity isn't relative to their lives. Most of them have little real knowledge of it. They're all in the book as baptised Christians but you watch them in church on their wedding day! The vicar will be saying, "Stand here, kneel, rise, find page 22, do this, do that…" They'll be all at sea. They'll have about as much notion of what to do as if they were being married in a Buddhist temple; I can quite understand this because I don't believe either. It isn't just their generation, is it? It is mine – their parents' generation, too. We doubted – they ignore.

The village people communed with nature but the youngsters don't do this either. The old people think deeply. They are great observers. They will walk and see everything. They didn't move far so their eyes are trained to see the fine detail of a small place. They'll say, 'The beans are a bit higher on the stalk this year...' I help to run the school farm but I'd never notice things like that. The old men can describe exactly how the ploughing turns over in a particular field. They recognize a beauty and it is this which they really worship. Not with words – with their eyes. Will these boys be like this when they are old? I'm just not sure. Nobody is trying to bring it out in them. Nobody says to them, 'This is heritage'. Somebody should be saying to them, "Let's go and *look*..."

Ronald Blythe
(b.1922)
AKENFIELD: <u>Portrait of an English Village</u>
(Contribution from the Teacher at the Agricultural Training Centre)

Maureen tried out her hair in different ways with her friend, Berna Lynch, and wore lipstick and powder when she was out of the house. Sixteen was a tiresome age to be in Kilgarret. There was nothing for young people: instead they were watched with suspicion, as if they were on probation from the age of sixteen to twenty – and even longer if, by then, they hadn't settled into the role of 'walking out' decorously with a suitable person. There were no social occasions. Maureen and Berna were considered too respectable to go to the local dance, where messenger boys and maids went. Peggy went to the dance on Saturday nights, but she hated to be asked about it. It wasn't for the likes of Berna and Maureen, she kept saying. They'd hate it even if they managed to get there. They were too well born for the fun and glitter of a hot dance hall, but they weren't well-born enough for the tennis parties and supper parties of the people in the big houses. There were the Wests and the Grays and the Kents, all with young people of Maureen and Berna's age, but they never met them. The children had been in boarding schools in Dublin; they came home at the end of term to the railway station three miles away, sometimes they arrived on the bus in the square with their lacrosse sticks and suitcases and blazers. Families in station-wagons met them with cries of excitement, but they never mixed in the life of the town.

Berna, as a doctor's daughter, could have been their social equal... but for all their gentility, it was known that her father had a problem with the drink. It was well hidden, but well known at the same time. So Berna missed her chance. Sweet little thing – such a pity about her father. Awfully good doctor, of course, but inclined to go off on his own and mixing with all kinds of rough people. Then into a nursing home in Dublin and after that he wouldn't touch the stuff for about eight months...

They were bored at the convent, they thought the other girls silly and parochial. The time passed very slowly while they waited for Maureen to be called for interview to the hospital and for Berna to go to a secretarial college in Dublin. Meanwhile, they sorted out their hair and their skin... and hoped that they would have some experience of something before they got to Dublin and everyone considered them real eejits.

Maeve Binchy
(b.1940)

LIGHT A PENNY CANDLE

Clare to his wife

O, once I had a true love,
As blest as I could be:
Young Patty was my turtle-dove,
And Patty she loved me.
We walked the fields together,
By wild roses and woodbine,
In summer's sunshine weather,
And Patty she was mine.

We stopped to gather primroses,
And violets white and blue,
In pastures and green closes
All glistening with the dew.
We sat upon green mole-hills,
Among the daisy flowers,
To hear the small birds' merry trills,
And share the sunny hours.

The blackbird on her grassy nest
We would not scare away,
Who nuzzling sat wi' scorchin' breast
On her eggs for half the day.
The chaffinch cheeped on the whitethorn,
And a pretty nest had she;
The magpie chattered all the morn
From her perch upon the tree.

And I would go to Patty's cot
And Patty came to mine;
Each knew the other's very thought
As birds at Valentine.
And Patty had a kiss to give,
And Patty had a smile,
To bid me hope and bid me live,
At every stopping stile.

We loved one summer quite away,
And then another came,
The cowslip close and sunny day,
It found us much the same.
We both looked on the selfsame thing,
Till both became as one;
The birds did in the hedges sing,
And happy time went on.

The brambles from the hedge advance,
In love wi' Patty's eyes:
On flowers, like ladies at a dance,
Flew scores of butterflies.
I claimed a kiss at every stile,
And had her kind replies.
The bees did round the woodbine toil,
Where sweet the small wind sighs.

John Clare
(1793 – 1864)

When George came back from the war Susan invited him to spend a weekend with her parents. He put on his demob suit, which didn't fit at all, and his demob tie which was wonderfully striped like a Neapolitan ice, and he succeeded in looking exactly what he wasn't, the gooping village bumpkin dressed up for a trip to town. We never heard what happened during that weekend; but it was clear enough that everything had gone wrong. When it was over George wrapped the precious demob suit away in tissue paper and put on his old paratroop's jacket again and went to work for William Hart. He lived at home with his parents and was able to save about two pounds a week out of his pay; and it was estimated that at this rate he would have saved two hundred in two years' time, with which in some mysterious way he would Better Himself and find favour in the eyes of Susan's parents. But in practice the sum didn't work out like that; for love makes nonsense of mathematics and George would have been a poor sort of lover if he hadn't been moved from time to time by the glory and splendour of his state to buy some absurd and prodigal present for Susan or to squander his week's savings recklessly on squiring all six of the Frolick Virgins to the Horse and Harrow and buying them gin. So it looked as if it might be ten years, rather than two, before George was able to afford to furnish a cottage let alone to Better Himself. Meanwhile the star-crossed pair continued to discover every imaginable delight in each other's company and to say goodnight to each other in an atmosphere of considerable drama outside the land girls' hostel every evening. Mr. Chorlton, who liked to walk in the garden at twilight and wrap himself in his thoughts, observed sadly that it was extremely difficult to concentrate while what appeared to be a combination of Troilus and Cressida, Pyramus and Thisbe, and Romeo and Juliet, breathed eternal farewells just outside the gate.

Anon Mrs. Merrythought, with much banging of bolts and

clanking of chains, would indicate that she was about to lock up and Susan would scuttle inside. But the lovers' parting was not for long; at seven o'clock next morning they would be reunited; for the land girls were hired out to various farmers in twos and threes and needless to say Susan generally contrived to be among those who worked for Mr. Hart. And so together, like characters in some ancient pastoral, the lovers mowed and reaped, ploughed and planted, and even discovered a kind of bliss in sprout-picking when they did it side by side. They were accessories to the crime, if it was one, of growing linseed in Little Twitlocks; for Susan had ploughed the field and George had sown the seed. As for old William, he was so crippled with rheumatism that he was only able to hobble as far as the gate and lean over it; but that was probably enough, for it was always said of him that he'd only got to look at something to make it grow.

John Moore
(1907 – 1967)

THE BLUE FIELD

One Sunday evening as I strolled down our village from Chapel, I met Olive. I had spoken to her before on the Evesham bus. There was something different about her speech as she walked, pushing her bike with me through three villages before I realised that I would have to walk all the way back home. It was just that a Private School had got rid of the Worcestershire burr, and as Uncle George would have said, she talked flash.

At the Roman Catholic Church corner she said as we parted, 'You can't kiss me tonight, but if we meet on Saturday you can.'

At tea-time on Saturday Mother sensed that, after a bath from the harvesting, the amount of Brylcream on my hair was above the usual and the shine of my shoes had an extra glow.

'Who are you seeing tonight then, Fred?' she asked, as I pushed my Hercules bike down the drive.

'Oh just someone I know a few villages away.'

Mother went back into our house and it was hard to say whether she was annoyed, amused or glad. I knew that she had hoped I'd marry Janet, the chubby Cheltenham girl, who used to sing solos at the Chapel and won prizes for her singing, but that was not to be.

'How about the flicks, say, at the Sabina at Tewkesbury, and can I call you Freddy?' Olive asked.

A new word to a village chap was 'flicks'. So we cycled to the town, had tea at a place known as the Ancient Grudge and to the flicks we went. Don't ask me what we saw, but I remember the red suede jacket and emerald green corduroy skirt which gave Olive an edge over the usual cinema goers of the town. Then the ride back with blacked out bicycle lamps under the stars. The halt at the roadside gate where Sunday's promise was kept and supper at her mother's hillside cottage and the promise of a meeting on Wednesday night.

Olive picked fruit from the trees planted by the famous Raymond Bush. Cox's Orange Pippins were weighing down the half-standard trees…

It's not usual for courting couples to judge their partner as they did years ago when the girl had to prove herself fit for a farmer's wife by lifting the heavy lid of the church chest, but I do recall vividly the muscles of my partner's arms. How strong they looked below the short sleeves of her Viyella shirt. 'The ground needs squeezlng hard like a young woman,' Jim Hicks always said. I suppose a young chap fancies his strength, but the days of fruit picking, the weeks of threshing corn, had given Olive a come-hither grip which was good to feel after the half-hearted embraces which we all go through.

It's true a girl who is warm-hearted and vivacious has something difficult to explain in words. The Bible says that there is nothing quite so wonderful as the way of a man with a maid. I would reverse that because the opposite sex have a disarming force which lifts a fellow like me high above the hill.

Fred Archer
(b.1915)

WHEN VILLAGE BELLS WERE SILENT

MARRIAGE AND PARENTHOOD

July ye 15. – Sarah was wed cum 4 days agon, and a right merrie time we did have. We, all up betimes, did work with a will to get all readie. Mistress Prue did get the tables all set in good time. John's mother helping, and all did look verrie well, there being great store of good things.

Then later we to help Sarah to put on her wedden cloes, it bein all new from shift to gown, and she did look verrie prettie

---

in her satin gown and wearing the gold necklace Cousin Ned did give her. Then Mistress Prue did fasten the wedden veil to her hair and she did look verrie daintie, like a real lady when readie to go to the Church.

We did make a goodlie show as we did walk down to the church, where Passon was waiting for us. John did father Sarah and did look verrie smart in his best velvet cloes. His mother did wear her grey silk, while I did put on my blue silk with the yellow lace.

Every boddie did cum to the church to see the wedden, and it ower we back home, all going off well at the church. Then the feasting did begin, and all did praise Mattie's way of doing the hares, and also Floe's little cakes.

There was much drinking of healths and speechifying. Then did cum a nice surprise for Sarah, for Carter's wife did cum to the parlour to say John was wanted, and he out, did cum back later to say it was a present cum for Sarah and she to go and see it.

So we all out with her to see whats agaite, and did see a man with a verrie prettie black ponie, which he did say was for Sarah from Mistress Ellis and Mary, and did give her a letter also, in which they did say the ponie was for her to ride with her new husband and that they did wish her much happiness and a long life.

Anne Hughes
(1885 – ?)

Diary of a Farmer's Wife, 1796-7

Nelly opened her eyes and through a crack in the brown curtains could glimpse the green of the hillside, patches of earth in the garden and bright sunlight on the bare apple tree. It was going to be a beautiful day. Quickly she sat up and looked to the light-brown costume hanging on the wall. Aunt Lizzie had made it for her and it was a professional job, elegant and sensible, better than a frilly white dress which had only one day's life in it and would then be closeted away. It could be worn as best for years after.

Nelly has forgotten everything that happened that morning until they came out of church. She was too excited to notice details and, since nothing went wrong, there was nothing to remember. She found herself hanging on tightly to Will's arm, standing in the sharp sunlight outside the church door, as a flock of birds fought excitedly for grains of rice among the tombstones. They walked to the church gate. The family were behind them, friends and neighbours along the path, and a little knot of children in front. She whispered, 'Have you got some coppers in your pocket, Will?' 'What do I want with coppers, Nelly?' he said. But of course, the gate was held fast closed by the grinning group of children. Will stopped and looked at them, nodding his head in understanding. He put his hand in his pocket and they all stopped chattering, but their grins grew even wider in anticipation. Then Will threw the coins high over their heads into the long grass. The gate was open, children vanished to scramble excitedly in the muddy tussocks. The way was clear. The wedding breakfast soon vanished. A crowd of guests took them down Station Hill to catch the four o'clock train and waved noisy 'good-byes' with white handkerchiefs as they drew out of the station. Will and Nelly sank into their seats and sighed with exhaustion. The train began to gather speed and whistled down the Ribble Valley, through cotton towns, into the world of red brick, past rows of terrace houses with back yards and coal sheds, alongside mills, mines and chimneys by the dozen. Nelly hardly spoke and Will closed his eyes, but whenever the train stopped at a station they smiled at each other. At length it let them down on the flat coastland by a vast shallow bay in Morecambe.

They would have four whole days on their own; Pancake Tuesday was almost over, but Ash Wednesday, Fritters Thursday, Fish Friday and Anything-you-like Saturday, remained. They walked to the boarding-house. Annie had booked it for them. They lived retiringly and never confessed to be newly married. Will would take a walk in the mornings while Nelly sat knitting. In the afternoons they walked along the promenade and looked at the sea. It was just like being a regular married couple. They had fine cold weather to blow colour into their cheeks, and the four days passed almost instantly. On Sunday morning, as they were about to leave, it began to rain. The landlady saw them to the door and wished Mr & Mrs Mason a good trip back home. On the doorstep Nelly unfastened her umbrella and pushed it up. Out fell a cascade of confetti over Nelly, Will and the landlady. 'Why,' said the landlady, 'Mrs Mason you've coloured up.' 'I'll colour me brother up too when I get home,' said Nelly.

Roger Mason
(b.1940)

Granny's Village

Clym and Eustacia, in their little house at Alderworth, beyond East Egdon, were living on with a monotony which was delightful to them. The heath and changes of weather were quite blotted out from their eyes for the present. They were enclosed in a sort of luminous mist, which hid from them surroundings of any inharmonious colour, and gave to all things the character of light. When it rained they were charmed, because they could remain indoors together all day with such a show of reason; when it was fine they were charmed, because they could sit together on the hills. They were like those double stars which revolve round and round each other, and from a distance appear to be one. The absolute solitude in which they lived intensified their reciprocal thoughts; yet some might have said that it had the disadvantage of consuming their mutual affections at a fearfully prodigal rate. Yeobright did not fear for his own part; but recollection of Eustacia's old speech about the evanescence of love, now apparently forgotten by her, sometimes caused him to ask himself a question; and he recoiled at the thought that the quality of finiteness was not foreign to Eden.

Thomas Hardy
(1840 – 1928)

THE RETURN OF THE NATIVE

To return to Isaac Bawcombe. He was born, we have seen, in 1800, and began following a flock as a boy and continued as shepherd on the same farm for a period of fifty-five years. The care of sheep was the one all-absorbing occupation of his life, and how much it was to him appears in this anecdote of his state of mind when he was deprived of it for a time. The flock was sold and Isaac was left without sheep, and with little to do except to wait from Michaelmas to Candlemas, when there would be sheep again at the farm. It was a long time to Isaac, and he found his enforced holiday so tedious that he made himself a nuisance to his wife in the house. Forty times a day he would throw off his hat and sit down, resolved to be happy at his own fireside, but after a few minutes the desire to be up and doing would return, and up he would get and out he would go again. One dark cloudy evening a man from the farm put his head in at the door. 'Isaac,' he said, 'there be sheep for 'ee up 't the farm – two hunderd ewes and a hunderd more to come in dree days. Master, he sent I to say you be wanted.' And away the man went.

Isaac jumped up and hurried forth without taking his crook from the corner and actually without putting on his hat! His wife called out after him, and getting no response sent the boy with his hat to overtake him. But the little fellow soon returned with the hat – he could not overtake his father!

He was away three or four hours at the farm, then returned, his hair very wet, his face beaming, and sat down with a great sigh of pleasure. 'Two hunderd ewes,' he said, ' and a hunderd more to come – what d'you think of that?'

'Well, Isaac,' said she, 'I hope thee'll be happy now and let I alone.'

W.H. Hudson
(1841 – 1922)

A SHEPHERD'S LIFE

For ten minutes the mother sat herself down, thinking of the condition of her youngest daughter, and trying to think what words she would use when she found herself in her daughter's presence. Sorrow, and Shame, and Sin! Her child a castaway! What terrible words they were! And yet there had been nothing that she could allege in answer to them. That comfortable idea of a decent husband for her child had been banished from her mind almost before it had been entertained. Then she thought of Rachel's eyes, and knew that she would not be able to assume a perfect mastery over the girl. When the ten minutes were over she had made up her mind to nothing, and then she also took up her candle and went to her room. When she first entered it she did not see Rachel. She had silently closed the door and come some steps within the chamber before her child showed herself from behind the bed. 'Mamma', she said, 'put down the candle that I may speak to you.' Whereupon

Mrs. Ray put down the candle, and Rachel took hold of both her arms. 'Mamma, you do not believe ill of me; do you? You do not think of me the things that Dorothea says? Say that you do not, or I shall die.'

'My darling, I have never thought anything bad of you before.'

'And do you think bad of me now? Did you not tell me before I went out that you would trust me, and have you so soon forgotten your trust? Look at me, mamma. What have I ever done that you should think me to be such as she says?'

'I do not think that you have done anything; but you are very young, Rachel.'

'Young, mamma! I am older than you were when you married, and older than Dolly was. I am old enough to know what is wrong. Shall I tell you what happened this evening? He came and met us all in the fields. I knew before that he had come back, for the girls had said so, but I thought that he was in Exeter when I left here. Had I not believed that, I should not have gone. I think I should not have gone.'

'Then you are afraid of him?'

'No, mamma; I am not afraid of him. But he says such strange things to me; and I would not purposely have gone out to meet him. He came to us in the fields, and then we returned up the lane to the brewery, and there we left the girls. As I went through the churchyard he came there too, and then the sun was setting, and he stopped me to look at it; I did stop with him, – for a few moments, and I felt ashamed of myself; but how was I to help it? Mamma, if I could remember them I would tell you every word he said to me, and every look of his face. He asked me to be his friend. Mamma, if you will believe in me I will tell you everything. I will never deceive you.'

She was still holding her mother's arms while she spoke. Now she held her very close and nestled in her bosom, and gradually got her cheek against her mother's cheek, and her lips against her mother's neck. How could any mother refuse such a caress as that, or remain hard and stern against such signs of love? Mrs. Ray, at any rate, was not possessed of strength to do so. She was vanquished, and put her arm round her girl and embraced her. She spoke soft words, and told Rachel that she was her dear, dear dearest darling. She was still awed and dismayed by the tidings which she had heard of the young man; she still thought there was some terrible danger against which it behoved them all to be on their guard. But she no longer felt herself divided from her child, and had ceased to believe in the necessity of those terrible words which Mrs. Prime had used.

'You will believe me?' said Rachel. 'You will not think that I am making up stories to deceive you?' Then the mother assured the daughter with many kisses that she would believe her.

Anthony Trollope
(1815 – 1882)

Rachel Ray

'So you consider my comfort,' said Mrs. Whelpdale. 'I suppose it's true. My daughter might do that.'

'I'm sure she does,' answered Sally.

'From a distance. Close at hand, it nauseates her. I never knew any young lady so soon bored. Where is she now?'

They could see Hermione, strolling ahead of them between two of the visiting cricketers. She was in a much-frilled, pouting bosomed, pale blue silk dress which was built high at the hips, and she walked with a lovely long-legged grace which, with her golden curls and blue eyes, moved Sally to a ruefulness approaching despair. Over her shoulder she carried as a toy a long-handled frilly sunshade of similar blue.

'There, ma'am,' said Sally raising her hand for an instant's indication.

Mrs. Whelpdale peered forward as if she were more short-sighted than she was. Her fingers pinched Sally's shoulder.

'Elegant, self-infatuated creature,' she said in a low voice. 'As I was at her age. Do you think her pretty, Sarah?'

'Very, ma'am,' said Sally.

'I was beautiful. And as great a fool.'

'Do you love my daughter, Sarah?'

'Yes, ma'am.'

'As if you meant it, too! Wonderful! But what else could you say? She doesn't love me. She's always in haste to leave me.'

'You send her away, ma'am.'

'Who? I? Don't be obstinate, child! I see your mouth. She adores her father. Victor loves me, in spite of...' Mrs. Whelpdale grew dark with thought. A moment later, she cried impetuously: 'Never marry, Sarah! It's madness. It drives one mad. Ah, I see you mean to do so, for all I say. So does Hermione. To get away from me. I think.'

Frank Swinnerton
(1884 – 1982)

ENGLISH MAIDEN

'Oh, daddy!' she cried, ' dear, good daddy! I don't want you to buy me a donkey, I want you to buy me a horse.'

'That's modest!' said the Squire; 'but what are you crying for?'

'Oh, it's such a poor horse! Such a very old, poor horse!' cried Amabel.

And from the window Mr. Ammaby was able to confirm her statements. It was the Cheap Jack's white horse, which he had been trying to persuade the landlord to buy as a cab-horse. More lean, more scarred, more drooping than ever, it was a pitiful sight, now and then raising its soft nose and intelligent eyes to the window, as if it knew what a benevolent little being was standing on a slippery chair, with her arms round the Squire's neck, pleading its cause.

'But when I buy horses,' said the Squire, 'I buy young, good ones, not very old and poor ones.'

'Oh, but do buy it, daddy! Perhaps it's not had enough to eat, like that kitten I found in the ditch. And perhaps it'll get fat, like her; and mamma said we wanted an old horse to go in the cart for luggage, and I'm sure that one's very old. And that's such a horrid man, like hump-backed Richard. And when nobody's looking he tugs it, and beats it. Oh, I wish I could beat him!' and Amabel danced dangerously upon the horsehair seat in her white gaiters, with impotent indignation.

The Squire was very weak when pressed by his daughter, but at horses, if at anything, he looked with an eye to business. To buy such a creature would be ludicrous. Still, Amabel had made a strong point by what Lady Louisa had said. No one, too, knew better than the Squire what a difference good and bad treatment can make in a horse, and this one had been good once, as his experienced eye told him. He said he 'would see,' and strolled into the yard.

Juliana Ewing
(1841 – 1885)

Jan of the Windmill

'Are they your children?' asked Yvette, rising from the fire and turning to the man.

He looked her in the eyes, and nodded.

'But where's your wife?'

'She's gone out with the basket. They've all gone out, cart and all, selling things. I don't go selling things. I make them, but I don't go selling them. Not often. I don't often.'

'You make all the copper and brass things?' she said.

He nodded, and again offered her the stool. She sat down.

'You said you'd be here on Fridays,' she said. 'So I came this way, as it was so fine.'

'Very fine day!' said the gipsy, looking at her cheek, that was still a bit blanched by the cold, and the soft hair over her reddened ear, and the long, still mottled hands on her knee.

'You get cold, riding a bicycle?' he asked.

'My hands!' she said, clasping them nervously.

'You didn't wear gloves?'

'I did, but they weren't much good.'

'Cold comes through,' he said.

'Yes!' she replied.

The old woman came slowly, grotesquely down the steps of the Caravan, with some enamel plates.

'The dinner cooked, eh?' he called softly.

The old woman muttered something, as she spread the plates near the fire. Two pots hung from a long iron horizontal bar, over the embers of the fire. A little pan seethed on a small iron tripod. In the sunshine, heat and vapour wavered together.

He put down his tools and the pot, and rose from the ground.

'You eat something along of us?' he asked Yvette, not looking at her.

'Oh, I brought my lunch,' said Yvette.

'You eat some stew?' he said. And again he called quietly, secretly to the old woman, who muttered in answer, as she slid the iron pot towards the end of the bar.

'Some beans, and some mutton in it,' he said.

'Oh, thanks awfully!' said Yvette. Then, suddenly taking courage, added: 'Well, yes, just a very little, if I may.'

She went across to untie her lunch from her bicycle, and he went up the steps to his own caravan. After a minute, he emerged, wiping his hands on a towel.

'You want to come up and wash your hands?' he said.

'No, I think not,' she said. 'They are clean.'

He threw away his wash-water, and set off down the road with a high brass jug, to fetch clean water from the spring that trickled into a small pool, taking a cup to dip it with.

When he returned, he set the jug and cup by the fire, and fetched himself a short log, to sit on. The children sat on the floor, by the fire, in a cluster, eating beans and bits of meat with spoon or fingers. The man on the log ate in silence, absorbedly. The woman made coffee in the black pot on the tripod, hobbling upstairs for the cups. There was silence in the camp. Yvette sat on her stool, having taken off her hat and shaken her hair in the sun.

'How many children have you?' Yvette asked suddenly.

'Say five,' he replied slowly, as he looked up into her eyes.

D.H. Lawrence
(1885 – 1930)

THE VIRGIN AND THE GYPSY

OLD AGE AND DYING

She told how they used to form for the country dances
'The Triumph', 'The New-rigged Ship' –
To the light of the guttering wax in the panelled manses,
And in cots to the blink of a dip.

She spoke of the wild 'poussetting' and 'allemanding'
On carpet, on oak, and on sod,
And the two long rows of ladies and gentlemen standing,
And the figures the couples trod.

She showed us the spot where the maypole was yearly planted,
And where the bandsmen stood
While breeched and kerchiefed partners whirled, and panted
To choose each other for good.

She told of that far-back day when they learnt astounded
Of the death of the King of France;
Of the Terror; and then of Bonaparte's unbounded
Ambition and arrogance.

Of how his threats woke warlike preparations
Along the southern strand,
And how each night brought tremors and trepidations
Lest morning should see him land.

She said she had often heard the gibbet creaking
As it swayed in the lightning flash,
Had caught from the neighbouring town a small child's shrieking
At the cart-tail under the lash...

With cap-framed face and long gaze into the embers –
We seated around her knees –
She would dwell on such dead themes, not as one who
remembers
But rather as one who sees.

She seemed one left behind of a band gone distant
So far that no tongue could hail:
Past things retold were to her as things existent,
Things present but as a tale.

Thomas Hardy
(1840 – 1928)

Sarah was flitting in and out of the cottage a long way up, taking observations with an old brass telescope. There is one little bit of road she watches for hours for the baker's cart.

Truly a habitation in the mountains of the moon. It is an exquisite view...

Sarah was fiddling about in the wet grass, very tall and upright, showing a worn and eager face at one end, and a pair of buttoned town boots at the other. She always reminds me somehow of a broom stick, a very pathetic one, poor Sarah.

She was in much better spirits than last time, when she seemed so overcome with the unaccustomed sight that she could only stare at us and mop her face. She explained naively that she had thought of so many things after we had gone, and proceeded to put questions again, which already she had unconsciously heard answered.

She had some lodgers from Fife, an absorbing event in their little world, and of no slight importance financially. I am afraid Duncan can earn very little now, and it is a poor cottage, and there is a certain soreness in having had to leave Tullymet.

Sarah is not so much altered, but very old. The same blinking eyes looking over her chin, and the same tone of voice, especially when she manages a laugh. There was a Scotch clip here and there, but the accent was English, and Lancashire at that, over the hills at the edge of the Derbyshire peak.

She has never been home or seen a relation since she married Duncan in '72 and when we came to her in June, we were the first visible travellers from her old outside world that had reached her since our other visit eight years ago – 'when you have a house there would be nobody to look after Duncan – and the hens' – there will be few left to visit if the delay lasts much longer.

Her sister, old Hannah is still alive, but must be very old. She was like a mumbling shrivelled old mummy when my grandmother died. Betty was the eldest sister, they must have been connected with the Leeches in service for a great while back, but I don't think they ever worked in Leech's Mill.

Sarah was kitchen maid, and then my mother's cook. We were at Tullymet for one summer '70, and she came back from London to marry the gamekeeper. I remember being taken up into the attic as a child to finger her lilac silk dress. He was a fine looking man, and she had £200 of savings. I am glad to say she has this yet, my father being one trustee, but I should think the income is very bare.

I never heard anything unsatisfactory of the gracious Duncan, but he has become slow, and he looks like a tough sort of old man who might last for ever on a little meal. They have no family. She became a Catholic, after a fashion, when she married him.

If Sarah ever showed any reserve when she was gamekeeper's wife at Tullymet, it is visited on her now in her inferior rank, but the situation has probably always been beyond her control. The Scotch are friendly to a friendly English family with ready money, but an unprotected stranger is a stranger to the bitter end – although they take him in. The loneliness must be all the more appalling when every one is cousins and a Clan.

Beatrix Potter
(1866 – 1943)

THE JOURNAL OF BEATRIX POTTER, 1881–1897
Monday, October 3rd, 1892

Mrs Jennings, Lady Middleton's mother, was a good-humoured, merry, fat, elderly woman, who talked a great deal, seemed very happy, and rather vulgar. She was full of jokes and laughter, and before dinner was over had said many witty things on the subject of lovers and husbands; hoped they had not left their hearts behind them in Sussex, and pretended to see them blush whether they did or not.

Mrs Jennings was a widow with an ample jointure. She had only two daughters, both of whom she had lived to see respectably married, and she had now, therefore, nothing to do but to marry all the rest of the world. In the promotion of this object she was zealously active, as far as her ability reached; and missed no opportunity of projecting weddings among all the young people of her acquaintance. She was remarkably quick in the discovery of attachment, and had enjoyed the advantage of raising the blushes and vanity of many a young lady by insinuations of her power over such a young man; and this kind of discernment enabled her, soon after her arrival at Barton, decisively to pronounce that Colonel Brandon was very much in love with Marianne Dashwood. She rather suspected it to be so, on the very first evening of their being together, from his listening so attentively while she sang to them; and when the visit was returned by the Middletons dining at the cottage, the fact was ascertained by his listening to her again. It must be so. She was perfectly convinced of it. It would be an excellent match, for he was rich and she was handsome. Mrs. Jennings had been anxious to see Colonel Brandon well married, ever since her connection with Sir John first brought her to her knowledge; and she was always anxious to get a good husband for every pretty girl.

The immediate advantage to herself was by no means inconsiderable, for it supplied her with endless jokes against them both. At the Park she laughed at the colonel, and in the cottage at Marianne. To the former her raillery was probably, as far as it regarded only himself, perfectly indifferent; but to the latter it was at first incomprehensible; and when its object was understood, she hardly knew whether most to laugh at its absurdity, or censure its impertinence; for she considered it as an unfeeling reflection on the colonel's advanced years, and on his forlorn condition as an old bachelor.

Jane Austen
(1775 – 1817)

Sense and Sensibility

His small house looks down over the harbour and from the kitchen window he has seen many of the changes. When he was young it was all sail except for the small coasters that brought in coal. Today there is still plenty of sail – the pleasure boats that jam the harbour in summer.

He has detailed knowledge of local conditions and will recite the names of every harbour and port along a two hundred mile stretch of coast. He is consulted about wind and tides, the sky at night, the names of ships, local regattas and anything to do with fishing.

The sea seems to have moulded him; his eyes are watery blue and he has the massiveness of some great sea animal. He still leads an active life, and can be seen most days at the harbour. If his familiar figure was not there people would be afraid that something was wrong. 'Where's Johnny?' they would ask, as if the sun or moon was absent.

Peter Somerville-Large
(b.1928)

CAPPAGHLAS

Reuben himself was still able for a great deal of work. Though over sixty, he still had much of the vigour, as he had all the straightness, of his youth. Work had not bent him and crippled him, as it had crippled Beatup, his junior by several years. The furnace of his pride and resolution seemed to have dried the damps steamed up by the earth from her revengeful wounds, so that rheumatism − the plague of the labourer on the soil − had done no worse for him than shooting pains in the winter with a slight thickening of his joints.

His hair had been grey for years, and as he grew older it did not whiten, but stayed the colour of polished iron, straight, shining, and thick as a boy's. He had lost two back teeth, and made a tremendous fuss about them, saying it was all the fault of the dentist in Rye, who preferred a shilling extraction to a threepenny lotion − but the rest of his teeth were as good as ever, though at last a trifle discoloured by smoking.

His face was a network of wrinkles. He was not the sort of countryman whose skin old age stretches smoothly over the bones and reddens benignly as a sun warmed apple. On the contrary, he had grown swarthier with the years, the ruddy tints had been hardened into the brown, and from everywhere, from the corners of his eyes, of his mouth, of his nose, across his forehead, along his cheeks, under his chin, spread a web of lines, some mere hair-tracery on the surface, others wrinkled deep, others ploughed in like the furrows of his own fields.

Sheila Kaye-Smith
(1887 - 1956)

Sussex Gorse

When I heard that my great-uncle Silas was dying, I did not believe it. He was so old that it had always been hard for me to realise that he had ever been born. It had always seemed to me that he had simply turned up, very old and imperishable with his crimson neckerchief and his bloodshot eye as bright as the neckerchief, his earth-coloured breeches, his winey breath and that huskily devilish voice that had told me so many stories and had left as many tantalizingly half-told. Yet I remember how he would often tell me that he could recollect – the word was his own – standing in a corn sheaf, in his frocks, and sucking at the breast his mother slipped out of her dress and held down for him in the harvest-field. "They had the titty, them days, till they were damn near big enough to reap and tie." Though he might very well have made it up. "I was allus tidy thursty", he would say at the end of that story, in fact at the end of any story, "Mouthful o' wine?" he would say. It was his favourite phrase.

It was early autumn, in the middle of harvest, when I heard that he was dying. If it had been winter or even spring, I might have believed it. But in autumn and at harvest it was unthinkable, absurd. His late peas would be coming into pod; for seventy years he had reckoned on them, without fail, for a last blow-out with a goose and a dish of apple sauce made from his own first cookers, on Michaelmas Sunday. Who would pick the peas and gather the apples and lard the goose if he were to die?

His potatoes would be dead ripe, the pears would be dripping into the golden orchard as mellow as honey, the elderberries would be drooping over the garden-hedge in grape-dark bunches, ripe for wine. What would happen to them if Silas died? What could happen? No one else could dig those potatoes or garner those pears or work that wine as he did. The very words "Silas is dying" seemed fantastic.

When the news came that he was dying .. I did not trouble to go over to see him. In imagination I saw him digging his potatoes in the hot September sun or mowing the half acre of wheat he grew every other year at the end of the paddock, 'just so I shan't forget how to swing a scythe'. The wheat kept him in bread, which he baked himself. He sent me a loaf sometimes, its crust as crisp as a wheat-husk and a dark earth colour, and I often went over to help him band and carry the wheat. Even when I heard he was dying I expected every day to hear he had mown the wheat and was ready for me. I took as little notice of the news as that.

But unexpectedly there came other news: 'They say Silas doesn't know what he's doing-half the time.' Not 'Silas is ill', or 'Silas is dying', or even 'Silas is unconscious', but 'Silas doesn't know what he's doing'. The words were ominous, a contradiction of my Uncle Silas's whole life, his principles, his character, his amazing cunning, his devilish vitality. They perturbed me, for they could mean so much. They might mean that my Uncle Silas had so changed that he now no longer knew beer from water or wheat from beans, that he had dug his potatoes under-ripe or carried his wheat wet or made his wine from green elderberries. If it meant these things then it also meant the end. For what separated my Uncle Silas from other men was exactly this. He knew what he was doing. How often had I heard him say with a cock of his bloodshot eye and the most devilish darkness, 'I know what I'm doing, me boyo. I know what I'm doing.'

The day after hearing the news I went over to see him.

H.E. Bates
(1905 - 1974)

My Uncle Silas

James Blake had never suffered from any illness, nor needed the care of a doctor. It was by an accident that he found his death in the end. A young mare stumbled and threw him on the highroad, a little way from his house. The neighbours carried him home and murmured to each other that a man of his years ought not to have gone riding on a young mare. But this was not James's own opinion. He had ridden many young mares, and saw no reason for being afraid of this one. Nor did Mrs Blake pay any heed to what the neighbours said. She spoke no words of rebellious grief, and expressed no vain regret, when the doctor told her that her husband had received internal injuries and could not live.

'It is the will of God,' she said, 'and what is to be must be, surely.'

After that she spoke no more on the subject. She sat and watched him, with no expression on her face except the usual one of wise, motherly calm. There is no wisdom to be got from books, or even from a man's wide experience of life, equal to that of a woman who has borne many children and reared them, who has for years which she had long ceased to reckon, been the partner of one man's successes and failures, sharer in many hopes and fears.

'The boys' returned from the hill field, and John, stepping softly, came into the room where his father lay.

'How's the work?' said James

'There's upwards of three ton in it,' said John,' and we'll get it saved dry if the weather holds, and that's what it's likely to do, for there's a heavy dew out and the wind was going round after the sun all day. You'll be pleased, so you will, when you see it.'

'I'll not see it,' said James.

'Don't be talking that way,' said John. 'Sure you'll be out looking at us by the time we have it in the tramp-cocks. What's to hinder you?'

'I'll not see it,' said James; 'but what does it matter if I don't, so long as it's a good crop and well saved?'

'Go on now to your tea, John,' said Mrs Blake, 'and don't be bothering your father. If it's the will of God for him to see the hay he'll see it.'

But James Blake was right. He saw little more on earth. For a while after John left he lay looking at his wife. Gradually the expression passed out of his eyes, and though they were still fixed on her she could not tell whether they saw her or not. At eight o'clock that evening Julia Mary stood beside him, and there was a momentary gleam of conscious recognition on his face. That passed too. Mrs Blake put her children out of the room and sat with him alone through the dim twilight of the summer night.

G A Birmingham
(1865 – 1950)
Irishmen All

Take the case of Job Ingram. He was such a quiet fellow, and a bit on the slow side, but liked by everyone. He cycled daily four miles to the glue factory and worked amid its stench uncomplainingly. He shovelled bones with a will and sometimes worked with his feet in a sea of maggots. Could such a man have a girlfriend who would meet him straight out of work, and love him unkempt and unwashed as he was? Well, to everyone's surprise, John did, and she was a good honest girl, too. Then one winter evening she met Job to 'call it off'. He lived with his widowed mother, and wouldn't marry while she was alive, and Nelly wouldn't wait any longer. Job's answer was swift and sure. He slashed both wrists with the pocket knife he used to carve his lunch with. When searchers from the village found him, it was too late.

Such incidents set everybody's conscience tingling. Job's funeral filled the church. Folks were saying they really wished they'd talked to Job a bit more and realised he could both love and be loved.

Harold Cramp
(b.1912)

Yeoman Farmer's Son

Chapter 2

CLASS

GENTRY AND LANDLORDS

Lady Lufton liked cheerful, quiet, well-to-do people, who loved their Church, their country, and their Queen, and who were not too anxious to make a noise in the world. She desired that all the farmers round her should be able to pay their rents without trouble, that all the old women should have warm flannel petticoats, that the working men should be saved from rheumatism by healthy food and dry houses, that they should all be obedient to their pastors and masters – temporal as well as spiritual. That was her idea of loving her country. She desired also that the copses should be full of pheasants, the stubble-field of partridges, and the gorse covers of foxes; in that way, also, she loved her country.

Anthony Trollope
(1815 – 1882)

FRAMLEY PARSONAGE

The dinner was exceedingly handsome, and there were all the servants, and all the articles of plate which Mr. Collins had promised; and, as he had likewise foretold, he took his seat at the bottom of the table, by her Ladyship's desire, and looked as if he felt that life could furnish nothing greater. He carved and ate and praised with delighted alacrity; and every dish was commended first by him, and then by Sir William, who was now enough recovered to echo whatever his son-in-law said, in a manner which Elizabeth wondered Lady Catherine could bear. But Lady Catherine seemed gratified by their excessive admiration, and gave most gracious smiles, especially when any dish on the table proved a novelty to them. The party did not supply much conversation. Elizabeth was ready to speak whenever there was an opening, but she was seated between Charlotte and Miss De Bourgh – the former of whom was engaged in listening to Lady Catherine, and the latter said not a word to her all dinner-time. Mrs. Jenkinson was chiefly employed in watching how little Miss De Bourgh ate, pressing her to try some other dish and fearing she was indisposed. Maria thought speaking out of the question, and the gentlemen did nothing but eat and admire.

When the ladies returned to the drawing-room, there was little to be done but to hear Lady Catherine talk, which she did without any intermission till coffee came in, delivering her opinion on every subject in so decisive a manner as proved that she was not used to have her judgment controverted. She inquired into Charlotte's domestic concerns familiarly and minutely, and gave her a great deal of advice as to the management of them all; told her how everything ought to be regulated in so small a family as hers, and instructed her as to the care of her cows and her poultry. Elizabeth found that nothing was beneath this great lady's attention which could furnish her with an occasion for dictating to others. In the intervals of her discourse with Mrs. Collins, she addressed a variety of questions to Maria and Elizabeth, but especially to the latter, of whose connections she knew the least, and who, she observed to Mrs. Collins, was a very genteel, pretty kind of girl. She asked her at different times how many sisters she had, whether they were older or younger than herself, whether any of them were likely to be married, whether they were handsome, where they had been educated, what carriage her father kept, and what had been her mother's maiden name? Elizabeth felt all the impertinence of her questions, but answered them very composedly.

Jane Austen
(1775 – 1817)

Pride and Prejudice

Its setting is the world of aristocratic country life during the first years of the Commonwealth. In some ways English high life does not seem to have altered much since then. Here we are in a country house. The gentlemen, just in from hunting, are starting to argue about politics; the ladies, bent over their needlework, gossip about the shocking conduct of Lady Mary Sandys in appearing publicly with her lover Colonel Paunton at Winchester Races. On the other hand we notice with surprise that they take it as quite natural that the gentlemen of their acquaintance should have been fighting a duel, and that they have all, so they say, been drinking beer at breakfast. Their dresses are not very clean; when a visitor comes in they sink to the ground in a magnificent curtsy; while in the corner of the room, a girl is writing to her lover in words of accomplished poetical eloquence. All this is not very like the high life we know.

Indeed, this society presents such a bewildering blend of the familiar and the unexpected that it is hard at first to get one's bearings in it. Its conditions of living were primitive and home-made. People remained for years together buried in the country, subsisting on food grown on their own land, and dwelling in houses built by their own workmen. Countesses superintended jam-making and counted the holes in their husbands' stockings; if the house was full of visitors, the hostess thought nothing of packing three ladies of title into one bed; the arrival of a new book was a rare event, only one uncertain post came and went in the week. People, most of them, were of a piece with the way they lived, normal, ingenuous, uninhibited, their interests revolving round the elemental facts of birth and death and marriage.

David Cecil
(1902 - 1986)

TWO QUIET LIVES

The man he had seen at the window was young Raleigh Pamment, the son and heir.

He had been sitting in an easy-chair, one leg over the arm busy with a memorandum book, a stump of pencil, and a disordered heap of telegrams, letters and newspapers.

Everybody writes to Mr Gladstone, a sort of human lion's mouth for post cards, but Raleigh junior had not got to manage the House of Commons, the revenue, the nation, the Turks, South Africa, the Nile, Ganges, Indus, Afghanistan, sugar, shipping, and Homer.

Yet Raleigh junior had an occasional table beside him, from which the letters, telegrams, newspapers, and scraps of paper had overflowed on to the floor. In a company's offices it would have taken sixteen clerks to answer that correspondence; this idle young aristocrat answered it himself, entered it in his day book, 'totted' it up, and balanced the – the residue.

Nothing at all businesslike, either, about him – nothing in the least like those gentlemen who consider that to go in to the 'office' every morning is the sum total of life. A most unbusinesslike young fellow.

A clay pipe in his mouth, a jar of tobacco on another chair beside him, a glass of whisky for a paper weight on his telegrams. An idle, lounging, 'bad lot'; late hours, tobacco, whisky, and ballet-dancers writ very large indeed on his broad face. In short, a young 'gent' of the latter half of the nineteenth century.

Not the slightest sign of 'blue blood' anywhere; not even in the cut of his coat, no Brummell-like elegance; hardly a Bond Street coat at all – rough, large, coarse cloth. If he had stood at the door of a shop he would have done very well indeed for a shopkeeper, the sort that drives about in a cart for orders .

Of his character nothing could be learned from his features. His face was broad, rather flat, with a short but prominent nose; in spite of indulgence, he kept a good, healthy, country colour. His neck was thick, his figure stout, his hands big – a jovial, good-tempered looking man.

His neck was very thick, tree-like; a drover's neck, no refinement or special intelligence indicated there; great power to eat, drink, and sleep – belly energy.

The Pamments were simply Englishmen, and liable to be born big, with broad faces, thick necks, and ultimate livers. It was no disgrace to Raleigh, that jolly neck of his.

Unless you are given to aesthetic crockery, or Francesco de Rimini, I think you would rather have liked him; a sort of fellow who would lend you his dogs, or his gun, or his horse, or his ballet-dancer, or his credit – humph! – at a moment's notice. But he was a very 'bad lot'; they whispered it even in dutiful Woolhorton.

Richard Jefferies
(1848 – 1887)

AMARYLLIS AT THE FAIR

He had been to see, that day, several orchards: one, the best in Kent; another, belonging to a millionaire, quite the worst; another, next door to the best and belonging to one of those expensive schools for select young gentlemen, next but one to the worst; and another, ten or fifteen miles away and belonging to a young man of independent means, bad enough.

His orchard was bad; no doubt of that. It had once been good and could, with intelligence and care, be good again. Of its apples, the Bramleys and Warners were still capable of large crops. There was, after all, as the expert pointed out, a war on and it was as wrong to neglect an orchard, the source of fruit, as to neglect a shell factory, the source of defence, attack, destruction or survival or however you like to put it. Here were thirty acres of Kentish land not being rightly used in time of war. To some of us it seemed like a time of revolution. What was the young man going to do?

The young man, it seemed, was going to do nothing. Am I right in thinking that his reason for doing nothing was typical not only of the man, but the class, the generation and the education from which he had come? I hope not. The reason for his doing nothing was that he had no money.

By which he meant, apparently, that he had too few sources of independent means. Money, for him, meant something unearned. Living on the land, not by it or for it, he contributed nothing at all to the social community of which he was part. Also he was going to do nothing because, really, he did not understand trees and because, anyway, he did not believe in pruning. An expensive education, to repeat which for his children was apparently his chief concern, had taught him to regard land as a pleasant appendage to a house, a protection for a view and a convenient place to shoot over on summer evenings and winter afternoons.

This young man is not alone. He is part of a tradition: a tradition connected with the great house, the big estate, the park-like, man-made, man-preserved scenery everywhere. He too, like them, is affected by the revolution, towards which he is contributing little. The revolt is being waged by others for many of whom he has a class contempt. He still dismisses servants with off-hand indifference, on the slightest pretext, turning them out of their cottages on the briefest possible notice, although the husbands and brothers of those same servants are in the revolt, fighting and perhaps dying in Libya, Malaya, on the sea, in the air or on the beaches of Dieppe. He has been brought up to regard humanity as divided into two classes, and not even three years of war have changed his view. To him the chief horror of war is that he has no money. It never occurs to him, apparently, to go out and, by the sweat of his hands, earn a little.

H.E. Bates
(1905 - 1974)

THE ENGLISH COUNTRYSIDE

He thus possessed a high sense of his pastoral vocation to the villagers of Ketteringham. The night when he arrived in Ketteringham after his continental tour, he said a prayer that he might be the father of the fatherless in the parish, the husband to the widow, a peacemaker and a teacher to the poor. He imagined himself to be 'the father of the parish', and used that phrase to describe himself. His ideals were best expressed in his record of the speech which he made to his tenants at the dinner to which he invited them on 13th February, 1854. 'I addressed them after on the comfort of living in Ketteringham, where they had a comfortable church – good school for the children – decent cottages and gardens at moderate rents or low ones – sure of being attended to if sick or find a friend if in want of one – and no man well-behaved out of employment at fair wages. Therefore they ought to be zealous, diligent, respectful workmen for their employers and kind to each other.' It was no empty word to say that he was the father of the parish. He built lodges at the entrances to the parks, cottages for his tenants and farmers and took trouble in teaching his tenants how to keep them neat and clean.

Owen Chadwick
(b.1916)

VICTORIAN MINIATURE

FARMERS AND MIDDLE CLASSES

'What a pretty room!' said Miss Matty, sotto voce.

'What a pleasant place!' said I, aloud, almost simultaneously.

'Nay! if you like it,' replied he; 'but can you sit on these great, black leather, three-cornered chairs? I like it better than the best parlour; but I thought ladies would take that for the smarter place.'

It was the smarter place, but, like most smart things, not at all pretty, or pleasant, or home-like; so, while we were at dinner, the servant-girl dusted and scrubbed the counting house chairs, and we sat there all the rest of the day.

We had pudding before meat; and I thought Mr Holbrook was going to make some apology for his old-fashioned ways, for he began –

'I don't know whether you like new-fangled ways.'

'Oh, not at all!' said Miss Matty.

'No more do I,' said he. 'My house-keeper will have these in her new fashion; or else I tell her that, when I was a young man, we used to keep strictly to my father's rule, 'No broth, no ball; no ball, no beef'; and always began dinner with broth. Then we had suet puddings, boiled in the broth with the beef: and then the meat itself. If we did not sup our broth, we had no ball, which we liked a deal better; and the beef which came last of all, and only those had it who had done justice to the broth and the ball. Now folks begin with sweet things, and turn their dinners topsy-turvy.'

When the ducks and green peas came, we looked at each other in dismay; we had only two-pronged, black-handled forks. It is true the steel was as bright as silver; but what were we to do? Miss Matty picked up her peas, one by one, on the point of the prongs, much as Aminé ate her grains of rice after her previous feast with the Ghoul. Miss Pole sighed over her delicate young peas as she left them on one side of her plate untasted, for they would drop between the prongs. I looked at my host: the peas were going wholesale into his capacious mouth, shovelled up by his large round-ended knife. I saw, I imitated, I survived! My friends, in spite of my precedent, could not muster up courage enough to do an ungenteel thing; and, if Mr

Holbrook had not been so heartily hungry, he would probably have seen that the good peas went away almost untouched.

After dinner, a clay pipe was brought in, and a spittoon; and, asking us to retire to another room, where he would soon join us, if we disliked tobacco-smoke, he presented his pipe to Miss Matty, and requested her to fill the bowl. This was a compliment to a lady in his youth; but it was rather inappropriate to propose it as an honour to Miss Matty, who had been trained by her sister to hold smoking of every kind in utter abhorrence. But if it was a shock to her refinement, it was also a gratification to her feelings to be thus selected; so she daintily stuffed the strong tobacco into the pipe, and then we withdrew. 'It is very pleasant dining with a bachelor,' said Miss Matty softly, as we settled ourselves in the counting-house. 'I only hope it is not improper; so many pleasant things are!'

Elizabeth Gaskell
(1810 – 1865)

CRANFORD

With this inspiriting notion, her questions increased in number and meaning; and she particularly led Harriet to talk more of Mr Martin, and there was evidently no dislike to it. Harriet was very ready to speak of the share he had had in their moonlight walks and merry evening games; and dwelt a good deal upon his being so very good-humoured and obliging. 'He had gone three miles round one day in order to bring her some walnuts, because she had said how fond she was of them, and in everything else he was so very obliging. He had his shepherd's son into the parlour one night on purpose to sing to her. She was very fond of singing. He could sing a little himself. She believed he was very clever, and understood everything. He had a very fine flock, and, while she was with them, he had been bid more for his wool than anybody in the country. She believed everybody spoke well of him. His mother and sisters were very fond of him. Mrs Martin had told her one day (and there was a blush as she said it) that it was impossible for anybody to be a better son, and therefore she was sure, whenever he married, he would make a good husband. Not that she wanted him to marry. She was in no hurry at all.'

'Well done, Mrs Martin!' thought Emma. 'You know what you are about.' 'And when she had come away, Mrs Martin was so very kind as to send Mrs Goddard a beautiful goose – the finest goose Mrs Goddard had ever seen. Mrs Goddard had dressed it on a Sunday and asked all the three teachers, Miss Nash, and Miss Prince, and Miss Richardson, to sup with her.'

'Mr Martin, I suppose, is not a man of information beyond the line of his own business? He does not read?'

'Oh, yes! – that is, no – I do not know – but I believe he has read a good deal – but not what you would think anything of. He reads the Agricultural Reports, and some other books that lay in one of the window seats – but he reads all <u>them</u> to himself.

But sometimes of an evening, before we went to cards, he would read something aloud out of the Elegant Extracts, very entertaining. And I know he has read the Vicar of Wakefield. He never read the Romance of the Forest, nor the Children of the Abbey. He had never heard of such books before I mentioned them, but he is determined to get them now as soon as ever he can.'

The next question was:

'What sort of looking man is Mr Martin?'

'Oh! not handsome – not at all handsome. I thought him very plain at first, but I do not think him so plain now. One does not, you know, after a time. But did you never see him? He is in Highbury every now and then, and he is sure to ride through every week in his way to Kingston. He has passed you very often.'

'That may be, and I may have seen him fifty times, but without having any idea of his name. A young farmer, whether on horseback or on foot, is the very last sort of person to raise my curiosity. The yeomanry are precisely the order of people with whom I feel I can have nothing to do. A degree or two lower, and a creditable appearance might interest me; I might hope to be useful to their families in some way or other. But a farmer can need none of my help, and is, therefore, in one sense, as much above my notice, as in every other he is below it.'

Jane Austen
(1775 – 1817)

EMMA

The large tenant farmer's social position was peculiar. Definitely he was not 'County'. There was a distinct line drawn between the owners of land, and those who rented it. But the 'County' met him as an equal over rural sport. In his own opinion the farmer was very superior to anyone in trade, I mean, the retail trade necessitating the trader keeping a shop, and, horror of horrors, serving behind its counter. To clean out a manure yard was a gentlemanly occupation by comparison. This is dying hard. You will still find in country districts tennis clubs and other societies which refuse membership to anyone who may be discovered during the week serving behind a shop counter, whilst farmers are accepted gladly.

Consequently the ruling house of the district gave three balls every season; one for their own friends, solely a 'County' affair, a tenants' ball, and a servants' ball, which last embraced the despised shopkeeper.

There were, of course, some unfortunate folk who did not fit into any of these balls, and some of them had the privilege or suffered the indignity of being invited to the last two.

Truly, the drawing of the various 'boundary' lines was a real and lively problem in rural circles.

A.G. Street
(1892 – 1966)

FARMER'S GLORY

Mrs Crawley did get up, and told Lucy that she was glad to see her, and Mr Crawley came forward, grammar in hand, looking humble and meek. Could we have looked into the innermost spirit of him and his life's partner, we should have seen that mixed with tbe pride of his poverty there was some feeling of disgrace that he was poor, but that with her, regarding this matter, there was neither pride nor shame. The realities of life had become so stern to her that the outward aspects of them were as nothing. She would have liked a new gown because it would have been useful; but it would have been nothing to her if all the county knew that the one in which she went to church had been turned three times. It galled him, however, to think that he and his were so poorly dressed. 'I am afraid you can hardly find a chair, Miss Robarts,' said Mr. Crawley.

'Ah! my friend,' said Mrs Crawley, taking hold of Mrs Robarts's arm and looking into her face, 'that sort of shame is over with me. God has tried us with want, and for my children's sake I am glad of such relief.'

'But will he be angry?'

'I will manage it. Dear Mrs Robarts, you must not be surprised at him. His lot is sometimes very hard to bear; such things are so much worse for a man than for a woman.' Fanny was not quite prepared to admit this in her own heart, but she made no reply on that head. 'I am sure I hope we may be able to be of use to you,' she said, 'if you will only look upon me as an old friend, and write to me if you want me. I hesitate to come frequently for fear that I should offend him.' And then, by degrees, there was confidence between them, and the poverty-stricken helpmate of the perpetual curate was able to speak of the weight of the burden to the well-to-do young wife of the Barchester prebendary. 'It was hard,' the former said, 'to feel herself so different from the wives of other clergymen around her – to know that they lived softly, while she, with all the work of her hands, and unceasing struggle of her energies, could hardly manage to place wholesome food before her husband and children. It was a terrible thing – a grievous thing to think of, that all the work of her mind should be given up to such subjects as these. But, nevertheless, she could bear it, she said, 'as long as he would carry himself like a man, and face his lot boldly before the world.' And then she told how he had been better there at Hogglestock than in their former residence down in Cornwall, and in warm language she expressed her thanks to the friend who had done so much for them.

When they were again in the pony carriage behind the impatient Puck, and were well away from the door, Fanny was first to speak. 'How very different those two are,' she said; 'different in their minds and in their spirit!'

'But how much higher toned is her mind than his! How weak he is in many things, and how strong she is in everything! How false is his pride, and how false his shame!'

'But we must remember what he has to bear. It is not every one that can endure such a life as his without false pride and false shame.'

'But she has neither,' said Lucy.

'Because you have one hero in a family, does that give you a right to expect another?' said Mrs Robarts.

Anthony Trollope
(1815 – 1882)

FRAMLEY PARSONAGE

My mother, though unworldly, was always attracted by the things of the world; she felt that if circumstances had been different she could have taken her place in it, but thanks to my father's preferring objects to people she had very little chance. She liked gossip, she liked social occasions and to be dressed right for them; she was sensitive to the public opinion in the village, and an invitation to some function in Salisbury would always see her a-flutter. To mix with well dressed people, on some smooth lawn, with the spire of the Cathedral soaring above, to greet and to be greeted by them, to exchange items of family news and make timid contributions to political discussions, all this gave her a tremendous pleasure; she felt supported by the presence of acquaintances; she needed a social frame. When the landau arrived (there was a lively stable in the village) she stepped into it with a little air of pride and self fulfilment very different from her usual diffident and anxious manner. And if she had persuaded my father to go with her, she would look almost triumphant.

L.P. Hartley
(1895 – 1972)

THE GO-BETWEEN

She was a woman of middle age, with well-formed features of the type usually found where perspicacity is the chief quality enthroned within … She had something of an estranged mien: the solitude exhaled from the heath was concentrated in this face that had risen from it. The air with which she looked at the heathmen betokened a certain unconcern at their presence, or at what might be their opinions of her walking in that lonely spot at such an hour, this indirectly implying that in some respect or other they were not up to her level. The explanation lay in the fact that though her husband had been a small farmer she herself was a curate's daughter, who had once dreamt of doing better things.

Persons with any weight of character carry, like planets, their atmospheres along with them in their orbits; and the matron who entered now upon the scene could, and usually did, bring her own tone into a company. Her normal manner among the heathfolk had that reticence which results from the consciousness of superior communicative power. But the effect of coming into society and light after lonely wandering in darkness is a sociability in the comer above its usual pitch, expressed in the features even more than in the words.

"Why, 'tis Mis'ess Yeobright,' said Fairway.

Thomas Hardy
(1840 – 1928)

RETURN OF THE NATIVE

PEASANTS AND LABOURERS

In a third case the attempt of a labouring man to live upon a small plot of land was successful – at least for some time. But it happened in this way. The land he occupied, about six acres, was situated on the outskirts of a populous town. It was moderately rented and of fairly good quality. His method could conveniently manage without having to pay too much for assistance – as a market garden. Being close to his customers, and with a steady demand at good prices all the season, this paid very well indeed. The remainder was ploughed and cropped precisely the same as the fields of larger farms. For these crops he could always get a decent price. The wealthy owners of the villas scattered about, some keeping as many horses as a gentleman with a country seat, were glad to obtain fresh fodder for their stables, and often bought the crops standing, which to him was especially profitable, because he could not well afford the cost of the labour he must employ to harvest them.

In addition, he kept several pigs, which were also profitable, because the larger part of their food cost him nothing but the trouble of fetching it. The occupants of the houses in the town were glad to get rid of the refuse, vegetables, etc; of these he had a constant supply. The pigs, too, helped him with manure. Next he emptied ash-pits in the town, and sifted the cinders; the better went on his own fire, the rest on his land. As he understood gardening he undertook the care of several gardens, which brought in a little money. All the rubbish, leaves, trimmings, etc., which he swept from the gardens he burnt, and spread the ashes abroad to fertilize his miniature farm.

In spring he beat carpets, and so made more shillings; he had also a small shed, or workshop, and did rough carpentering. His horse did his own work and occasionally that of others; so that in half a dozen different ways he made money independent of the produce of his land. That produce, too, paid well, because of the adjacent town, and he was able to engage assistance now and then. Yet, even with all these things, it was hard work, and required economical management to eke it out. Still it was done, and under the same conditions doubtless might be done by others. But then everything lies in those conditions. The town at hand, the knowledge of gardening, carpentering, and so on, made just all the difference.

Richard Jefferies
(1848 – 1887)

HODGE AND HIS MASTERS

In the country the vicar might help the poor by finding them allotments, perhaps on the glebe, but if he did this he was advised to make sure that certain conditions were first fulfilled. He must see to it that the local farmers had no objection to the scheme, and it was possible to achieve this if the amount of land made available for an allotment did not exceed what the holder of it, together with his family, could cultivate thoroughly with spade husbandry in their unoccupied and leisure hours. A rood was generally regarded as about the right amount of land if this requirement were to be met, and the land should be let at the same rate as it would be to a farmer, so that farmers could not complain of being treated less fairly than their workers. The creation of allotments, it was maintained, diminished drunkenness, made parishioners happier and more industrious, and helped them to climb several rungs of the social ladder if they showed prowess at cultivation. On light evenings, Flora Thompson recalled, the men, after a hard day's work in the fields and their tea-cum-supper in their cottages, would work strenuously in their gardens and allotments, while on moonlit nights in the spring the solitary fork of someone who had not been able to tear himself away from his land would be heard, and the man singing. The cottage gardens were kept for green vegetables and the pig; the allotments were usually divided into two and used, the one half for potatoes, the other for wheat or barley. If the land were glebe land, then the incumbent could insist that the tenant and his family attend divine service on Sundays and that they should on no account work on the land on that day. If the tenant were convicted of poaching, thieving, drunkenness, or any offence against the laws of the country, he must give up his lot at the Michaelmas ensuing. What spectacle so delightful, asked the Rev. John Sandford, 'as that of a healthy, industrious, contented and religious peasantry – men civilised and attached by the influence of kindness – whom you found rude, lawless and estranged, because neglected – but whom the sympathy of the superior has reformed and won; and who, instead of being a ready prey to the incendiary and the democrat, are the cheap and loyal defence of property and law?'

Peter C. Hammond

PARSON AND THE VICTORIAN PARISH

Enter Corin and Touchstone

Cor. And how like you this shepherd's life, Master Touchstone?

Touch. Truly, shepherd, in respect of itself, it is a good life, but in respect that it is a shepherd's life, it is naught. In respect that it is solitary, I like it very well; but in respect that it is private, it is a very vile life. Now in respect it is in the fields, it pleaseth me well; but in respect it is not in the court, it is tedious. As it is a spare life, look you, it fits my humour well; but as there is no more plenty in it, it goes much against my stomach. Hast any philosophy in thee, shepherd?

Cor. No more, but that I know, the more one sickens, the worse at ease he is; and that he that wants money, means, and content, is without three good friends; that the property of rain is to wet, and fire to burn; that good pasture makes fat sheep, and that a great cause of the night is lack of the sun; that he that hath learned no wit by nature nor art may complain of good breeding, or comes of a very dull kindred.

Touch. Such a one is a natural philosopher. Wast ever in court, shepherd?

Cor. No, truly.

Touch. Then thou art damned.

Cor. Nay, I hope, –

Touch. Truly, thou art damned, like an ill-roasted egg, all on one side.

Cor. For not being at court? Your reason.

Touch. Why, if thou never wast at court, thou never saw'st good manners: If thou never saw'st good manners, then thy manners must be wicked; and wickedness is sin, and sin is damnation. Thou art in a parlous state, shepherd.

Cor. Not a whit, Touchstone: those that are good manners at the court are as ridiculous in the country as the behaviour of the country is most mockable at the court. You told me, you salute not at the court, but you kiss your hands: that courtesy would be uncleanly, if courtiers were shepherds.

Touch. Instance, briefly: come, instance.

Cor. Why, we are still handling our ewes, and their fells, you know, are greasy.

Touch. Why, do not your courtier's hands sweat? and is not the grease of a mutton as wholesome as the sweat of a man? Shallow, shallow. A better instance, I say; come.

Cor. Besides, our hands are hard.

Touch. Your lips will feel them the sooner: Shallow again. A more sounder instance; come.

Cor. And they are often tarred over with the surgery of our sheep; and would you have us kiss tar? The courtier's hands are perfumed with civet.

Touch. Most shallow man! Thou worms-meat, in respect of a good piece of flesh, indeed! – Learn of the wise, and perpend: civet is of a baser birth than tar: the very uncleanly flux of a cat. Mend the instance, shepherd.

Cor. You have too courtly a wit for me: I'll rest.

Touch. Wilt thou rest damned? God help thee, shallow man! God make incision in thee! thou art raw.

Cor. Sir, I am a true labourer: I earn that I eat, get that I wear: owe no man hate, envy no man's happiness, glad of other men's good, content with my harm; and the greatest of my pride is, to see my ewes graze and my lambs suck.

Touch. That is another simple sin in you, to bring the ewes and the rams together, and to offer to get your living by the copulation of cattle; to be bawd to a bell-wether, and to betray a she-lamb of a twelve-month, to a crooked-pated, old, cuckoldy ram, out of all reasonable match. If thou be'st not damned for this, the devil himself will have no shepherds: I cannot see else how thou shouldst scape.

William Shakespeare
(1564 – 1616)

As You Like It

He looked and smelt like Autumn's very brother, his face being sunburnt to wheat-colour, his eyes blue as corn-flowers, his sleeves and leggings dyed with fruit-stains, his hands clammy with the sweet juice of apples, his hat sprinkled with pips, and everywhere about him that atmosphere of cider which at its first return each season has such an indescribable fascination for those who have been born and bred among the orchards. Her heart rose from its late sadness like a released bough; her senses revelled in the sudden lapse back to Nature unadorned. The consciousness of having to be genteel because of her husband's profession, the veneer of artificiality which she had acquired at the fashionable schools, were thrown off, and she became the crude country girl of her latent early instincts.

Thomas Hardy
(1840 - 1928)

THE WOODLANDERS

Labourer, soldier, labourer, tinker, umbrella man, he had always wandered, and knew the South Country between Fordingbridge and Dover as a man knows his garden. Every village, almost every farm-house, especially if there were hops on the land, he knew, and could see with his blue eyes as he remembered them and spoke their names. I never met a man who knew England as he did. As he talked of places his eyes were alight and turned in their direction, and his arm stretched out to point, moving as he went through his itinerary, so that verily, wherever he was, he seemed to carry in his head the relative positions of all the other places where he had laboured and drunk and lit his solitary fire. 'Was you ever at H__ ?' he said, pointing to the Downs, through which he seemed to see H__ itself. 'General__, that commanded us, lived there. He died there three years ago at the age of eighty-eight, and till he died I was always sure of a

HENRY
CROW.

half-crown if I called there on a Christmas Eve, as I generally managed to do.' Of any place mentioned he could presently remember something significant – the words of a farmer, a song, a signboard, a wonderful crop, the good ale – the fact that forty-nine years ago the squire used to go to church in a smock frock. All this time his face was moved with free and broad expressions as he thought and remembered, like an animal's face.

Edward Thomas
(1878 - 1917)

THE SOUTH COUNTRY

And this quiet acceptance of the situation, recognizing that he if anyone must suffer, and take the hard place which soils the clothes and shocks the feelings, gives the clue to the average labourer's temper. It is really very curious to think of. Rarely can a labourer afford the luxury of a 'change'. Wet through though his clothes may be, or blood-stained, or smothered with mud or dust, he must wear them until he goes to bed, and must put them on again as he finds them in the morning; but this does not excuse him in our eyes from taking the disagreeable place. Still less does it excuse him in his own eyes. If you offer to help, men of this kind will probably dissuade you. 'It'll make yer clothes all dirty,' they say; 'you'll get in such a mess'. So they assume the burden, sometimes surly and swearing, oftener with a good-tempered jest.

To anything with a touch of humour in it they will leap forward like schoolboys. I am reminded of a funny incident one frosty morning when patches of the highway were slippery as glass. Preceding me along the road was a horse and cart, driven by a boy who stood upright in the cart, and seemed not to notice how the horse's hooves were skidding; and some distance ahead three railway navvies were approaching, just off their night's work, and carrying their picks and shovels. I had left the cart behind, and was near these three when suddenly they burst into a laugh, exclaiming to one another, 'Look at the old 'oss!' I turned. There sat the horse on his tail between the shafts, pawing with his feet at the road, but unable to get a grip at its slippery surface. It was impossible not to smile; he had such an absurd look. The navvies, however, did more than smile. They broke into a run; they saw immediately what to do. In thirty seconds they were shovelling earth out from the hedgerow under the horse's feet, and in two minutes more he had scrambled up, unhurt.

George Bourne
(1863 - 1927)

CHANGE IN THE VILLAGE

The man who lives under that roof and was born there seventy years ago is like his house. He is short and immensely broad, black-haired, with shaved but never clean-shaven face creased by a wide mouth and long narrow black eyes – black with a blackness as of cold, deep water that had never known the sun but only the candle light of discoverers. His once grey corduroys and once white slop are stained and patched to something like the colour of the moist, channelled thatch and crumbling 'clunch' of the stone walls. He wears a soft felt hat with hanging broad brim of darker earthy hues; it might have been drawn over his face and ears in his emergence from his native clay and flint. Only rarely does his eye – one eye at a time – gloom out from underneath, always accompanied by a smile that slowly puckers the wrinkled oak-bark of his stiff cheeks. His fingers, his limbs, his face, his silence, suggest crooked oak timber or the gnarled stoles of the many times polled ash. It is barely credible that he grew out of a child, the son of a woman, and not out of the earth itself, like the great flints that work upwards and out on to the surface of the fields. Doubtless he did, but like many a ruined castle, like his own house, he has been worn to a part of the earth itself. That house he will never give up except by force, to go to workhouse or grave. They want him to go out for a few days that it may be made more weather-tight; but he fears the chances and prefers a rickety floor and draughty wall. He is half cowman, half odd–job man – at eight shillings a week – in his last days, mending hedges, cleaning ditches, and carrying a sack of wheat down the steep hill on a back that cannot be bent any farther. Up to his knees in the February ditch, or cutting ash–poles in the copses, he is clearly half converted into the element to which he must return.

Edward Thomas
(1878 – 1917)

THE SOUTH COUNTRY

In the cross lane below Tybella old deaf Tom Gore was mending a ruined dry stone wall. He said he had only one pair of boots in the world, they were cracked and full of holes and he had asked in vain of the relieving officer to beg the Board of the Guardians to give him a new pair. He told me his wife was ill and he hoped he should not lose her. He remembered what it was after he lost his first wife, how he often came home wet through to the skin and no fire and no food cooked. Four little children of his lay side by side in Bryngwyn Churchyard. He had seen trouble. He didn't know but he thought it was fate. I could scarcely make him understand a word. He went on building up his stone wall at half a crown a perch and I went on to see his wife.

Francis Kilvert
(1840 – 1879)

KILVERT'S DIARY

THE POOR

As for the drudgery, poor people, living in a village like ours, could never expect to get away from it. Without money, without some small influence, what hope was there? Not one in a hundred of farm labourers ever had the chance to be anything more. Those who did manage to crawl up the ladder, for a step or two, only did so by slaving practically night and day, and lying and cheating at every opportunity. There was talk, at times, of small holdings being made available, and the phrase 'three acres and a cow' was passed about, as if it was going to give the labourer a little independence some time. But Lord Postern wouldn't allow any of his farms to be cut up, and there wasn't any other land that was suitable, so the talk died out. It was hard to have any self respect when, at any minute, a man might be given the few shillings due to him, and told to clear off, and not ask for a reference because he wouldn't get one; and that meant no work, unless he could find something a long way away, and move out of the district altogether. A rough word, a back answer, might bring that at any time. Self respect wasn't easy, yet we wanted it so much that we had to have it somehow. 'Don't crawl to nobody,' Mother would say. 'Do your work, treat the gentry with respect, because that's right, they are the gentry, but don't let them wipe their shoes on you. People won't respect you for doing that. If you can't get on by honest means, don't get on by dishonest, the Lord never gave a blessing for that,' was what she taught us, over and over again, as children, striving to put into us the creed that sustained her; a creed compounded of her own resolute independence, and the church-going religion she had been brought up in. I could never make out why in novels and such things the poor were generally represented as squalid, or ridiculous. My parents were poor enough, God knows, but they were neither squalid, nor ridiculous. They seemed good people to me, as good as any people could be. My father had the patient courage of an animal, that bears, and endures, and gives of its strength, without pause, and with a quiet heart, because it is aware of nothing but the immediate effort. Mother had a courage of the spirit, something finer, and more capable of suffering. She not only felt the struggle of the moment, but also knew the bitter injustice of the life she led, which only her religion made endurable. The world was a harsh place, but she would defy whatever it might inflict upon herself, and give, what small help she could, to those who were even more hardly treated than she was. For her, kindness was an act of pity to the tortured human race, which needed pity so much and got so little.

Richard Hillyer
(? – 1981)

COUNTRY BOY

One day it was bitterly cold – 'shrammelling cold' – the bread was finished, every crumb, the two little ones, 'just clam o' hunger,' were lying on the hearthrug crying for more. There was an end of gammon hanging high up on the wall – now and again there was a bit of bacon for the Sunday dinner. The idea occurred to the adventurous Sammy, who the next week was to begin life as a rook-scarer, that if the bit of raw pig-meat could be got down from the wall, the crying of the fammelled babes on the floor might be stilled. He mounted a rickety chair on the table, and then clambered up upon it, and stretching out to reach the meat, toppled over. He lay on the floor motionless. The children wailed, the little girl rattled the closed door in vain. It grew dark, and Sammy lay there, still as a dead thing. 'Just then, as though the Almighty had heard us childern wailin', the key turned in the lock, and there was mother's voice right among us.' Sammy woke and said, 'I baint 'urted, mother, I baint 'urted.' But he did not move. Ee 'had no felth in either limb.' His back was broken, and he died in two or three days. We suppose the Rector, at the funeral of this child, said, several times over, 'Thy will be done' and 'Give us this day our daily bread.'

R L Gales
(1862 – 1927)

VANISHED COUNTRYFOLK

Then an old woman and a small child appeared in sight, both with enormous sun-bonnets and carrying baskets. As they came up with me the woman stopped and swept her face with her hand, while the child, depositing the basket in the dust with great care, wiped her little sticky fingers on her pinafore. Then the shady hedge beckoned them and they came and sat down near me. The woman looked about seventy, tall, angular, dauntless, good for another ten years of hard work. The little maid – her only grandchild, she told me – was just four, her father away soldiering, and the mother died in childbed, so for four years the child had known no other guardian or playmate than the old woman. She was not the least shy, but had the strange self possession which comes from associating with one who has travelled far on life's journey.

'I couldn't leave her alone in the house,' said her grandmother, 'and she wouldn't leave the kitten for fear it should be lonesome' – with a humorous, tender glance at the child – 'but it's a long tramp in the heat for the little one, and we've another mile to go.'

'Will you let her bide here till you come back?' I said. 'She'll be all right by me.'

The old lady hesitated.

'Will 'ee stay by him, dearie?' she said.

The small child nodded, drew from her miniature pocket a piece of sweetstuff, extracted from the basket a small black cat, and settled in for the afternoon. Her grandmother rose, took her basket, and, with a nod and 'Thank 'ee kindly, mister,' went off down the road...

Presently an old man came by, lame and bent, with gnarled twisted hands, leaning heavily on his stick.

He greeted me in a high, piping voice, limped across to the child, and sat down.

'Your little maid, mister?' he said.

I explained.

'Ah,' he said, 'I've left a little darlin' like this at 'ome. It's 'ard on us old folks when we're one too many; but the little mouths must be filled, and my son, 'e said 'e didn't see they could keep me on the arf-crown, with another child on the way; so I'm tramping to N _ to the House; but it's a 'ard pinch, leavin' the little ones.'

I looked at him — a typical countryman, with white hair, mild blue eyes, and a rosy, childish, unwrinkled face.

'I'm eighty-four,' he went on, 'and terrible bad with the rheumatics and my chest. Maybe it'll not be long before the Lord remembers me.'

The child crept close and put a sticky little hand confidingly into the tired old palm. The two looked strangely alike, for the world seems much the same to those who leave it behind as to those who have but taken the first step on its circular pathway...

The old man sat resting: I had promised him a lift with my friend the driver of the flour-cart, and he was almost due when the child's grandmother came down the road.

When she saw my other visitor she stood amazed.

'What, Richard Hunton, that worked with my old man years ago up at Ditton, whatever are you doin' all these miles from your own place?'

'Is it Eliza Jakes?'

He looked at her dazed, doubtful.

'An' who else should it be? Where's your memory gone, Richard Hunton, and you not such a great age either? Where are you stayin'?'

Shame overcame him; his lips trembled, his mild blue eyes filled with tears. I told the tale as I had heard it, and Mrs Jakes's indignation was good to see.

'Not keep you on 'alf a crown! Send you to the House! May the Lord forgive them! You wouldn't eat no more than a fair-sized cat, and not long for this world either, that's plain to see. No, Richard Hunton, you don't go to the House while I'm above ground; it'd make my good man turn to think of it. You'll come 'ome with me and the little 'un there. I've my washin', and a bit put by for a rainy day, and a bed to spare, and the Lord and the parson will see I don't come to want.'

She stopped breathless, her defensive motherhood in her arms.

The old man said quaveringly, in the pathetic, grudging phrase of the poor, which veils their gratitude while it testifies their independence, 'Maybe I might as well.' He rose with difficulty, picked up his bundle and stick, the small child replaced the kitten in its basket, and thrust her hand in her new friend's.

'Then 'oo is grandad tum back,' she said.

Mrs Jakes had been fumbling in her pocket, and extracted a penny, which she pressed on me.

'It's little enough, mister,' she said

Then as I tried to return it: 'Nay, I've enough, and yours is poor paid work.'

I hope I shall always be able to keep that penny; and as I watched the three going down the dusty white road, with the child in the middle, I thanked God for the Brotherhood of the Poor.

Michael Fairless
(1869 – 1901)

THE ROADMENDER

Chapter 3

CHURCH

CHURCH AND CHAPEL

'To hell with Wesley,' retorted [Archdeacon] Trusswell. 'I'll have him put in the River Avon.'

'The first time that I knowed you was in favour of adult baptism, Master Trusswell.'

'What did he tell my people on the village cross? Out with it man.'

'He told us that there was one mediator between God and man and that was not the Bishops, but Christ. He also told us to repent, which I have done.'

'Anything else, Smith?' the Archdeacon snorted as Burman the groom and coachman had some difficulty holding his horses.

'Yes, that we was all equal in the sight of God. Naked we comes into the world and naked we goes out.'

'Haven't I preached that very thing at St. Andrew's, you'll bear me out with that, Burman?'

'Yes, sir,' Burman said.

'Oi, we be about as equal as the rich man and Lazarus in the Bible. Stubbs read that out Sunday night.'

'What do you mean, Smith? I'm in a hurry but I'll listen.'

Abel Smith had never spoken man to man with the Archdeacon before; besides, the reverend gentleman also being chairman of the court, Abel felt he could be flung in jail. "Tis like this, sir. You talks of equality in the sight of God, now I be more or less satisfied with my work, Master Besford is very good to me, but when we come to church Sunday morning it be different. You takes the elements first at Communion, which is right, but what happens after? Fust it's Lord and Lady Waterford and Sir John Franklin in their warm pews by the stove, velvet cushions they sits on. Then comes the farmers, the wheelwrights, the baker, the cottage farmers and the strip holders with their grazing rights – they sits amust at the back on them hard cold pews. Then we few labourers, 'tis pitiful to see us, amus too ashamed to darken the door of God's house. Thur we sits on the bench by the door in our smock frocks and blackleaded hobnail boots, our heads bowed. Anant us sits the shepherds, their dogs chained to the pew ends when they be able to come. You a sin the pew and anant the door with the knobs on um amus worn away by the dog chains. We be perished. When we walks up to the holy table, we be so ashamed our yuds be bowed, no one spakes to us. Be us equal or no in God's sight? We be around the table at Stubbs in Ayshon Wood house.' Abel finished with these words:"'Tis hard for a rich man to enter the Kingdom of God.' Trusswell took the whip from the coachman and with his horses at the canter he left Abel Smith in the middle of the road.

Fred Archer
(b.1915)

HAWTHORN HEDGE COUNTRY

Honour had been shown to Mr. Tryan, not at all because Mrs. Jerome had any high appreciation of his doctrine or of his exemplary activity as a pastor, but simply because he was a 'Church clergyman,' and as such was regarded by her with the same sort of exceptional respect that a white woman who had married a native of the Society Islands might be supposed to feel towards a white-skinned visitor from the land of her youth. For Mrs. Jerome had been reared a Churchwoman, and having attained the age of thirty before she was married, had felt the greatest repugnance in the first instance to renouncing the religious forms in which she had been brought up. 'You know,' she said in confidence to her Church acquaintants, 'I wouldn't give no ear at all to Mr. Jerome at fust; but after all, I begun to think as there was a many things worse nor goin' to chapel, an' you'd better do that nor not pay your way. Mr. Jerome had a very pleasant manner with him, an' there was niver another as kept a gig, an' 'ud make a settlement on me like him, chapel or no chapel. It seemed very odd to me for a long while, the preachin' without book, an' the stannin' up to one long prayer, istid o' changin' your postur. But la! there's nothing' as you mayn't get used to i'time; you can al'ys sit down, you know, before the prayer's done. The ministers say pretty nigh the same things as the Church parsons, by what I could iver make out, an' we're out o' chapel i' the mornin' a deal sooner nor they're out o' church. An' as for pews, ours is a deal comfortabler nor any i' Milby Church'.

George Eliot
(1819 – 1880)

SCENES OF CLERICAL LIFE

Mr Puddleham had been much elated by the prospect of his new Bethel, and had, it must be confessed, received into his mind an idea that it would be a good thing to quarrel with the Vicar …

He was a much older man than Mr. Fenwick, having been for thirty years in the ministry, and he had always previously enjoyed the privilege of being on bad terms with the clergyman of the Establishment. It had been his glory to be a poacher on another's manor, to filch souls, as it were, out of the keeping of a pastor of a higher grade than himself, to say severe things of the shortcomings of an endowed clergyman, and to obtain recognition of his position by the activity of his operations in the guise of a blister. Our Vicar, understanding something of this, had, with some malice towards the gentleman himself, determined to rob Mr. Puddleham of his blistering powers. There is no doubt a certain pleasure in poaching which does not belong to the licit following of game; but a man can't poach if the right of shooting be accorded him. Mr. Puddleham had not been quite happy in his mind amidst the ease and amiable relations which Mr. Fenwick enforced upon him, and had long since began to feel that a few cabbages and peaches did not repay him for the loss of those pleasant and bitter things, which it would have been his to say in his daily walks and from the pulpit of his Salem, had be not been thus hampered, confined, and dominated. Hitherto he had hardly gained a single soul from under Mr. Fenwick's grasp, – had indeed on the balance lost his grasp on souls, and was beginning to be aware that this was so because of the cabbages and the peaches. He told himself that though he had not hankered after these flesh-pots, that though he would have preferred to be without the flesh-pots, he had submitted to them. He was painfully conscious of the

guile of this young man, who had, as it were, cheated him out of that appropriate acerbity of religion, without which a proselyting sect can hardly maintain its ground beneath the shadow of an endowed and domineering Church. War was necessary to Mr. Puddleham. He had come to be hardly anybody at all, because he was at peace with the vicar of the parish in which he was established. His eyes had been becoming gradually open to all this for years; and when he had been present at the bitter quarrel between the Vicar and the Marquis, he had at once told himself that now was his opportunity. When it was suggested to him by Mr. Packer, the Marquis's man of business, that the green opposite to the Vicarage gate would be a convenient site for his chapel, and that the Marquis was ready to double his before-proffered subscription, then he saw plainly that the moment had come and that it was fitting that he should gird up his loins and return all future cabbages to the proud donor.

Anthony Trollope
(1815 – 1882)

THE VICAR OF BULLHAMPTON

CLERGY AND CLERGY WIVES

Hawker was one of the great eccentrics of the last century. The son of a Plymouth doctor, he had, as a boy, dressed himself in seaweed and sat on a rock at Bude combing his long hair; a farmer took a shot at him but missed. Halfway through his career at Oxford he heard that his father could no longer support him, so he immediately proposed marriage to a lady twice his age, who had 'taught him his letters', and was accepted. As rector of Morwenstow, Hawker continued eccentric both in his dress and his behaviour. His habitual outfit, when visiting his parishioners, was a long-tailed claret-coloured coat with a yellow poncho over it, a blue fisherman's sweater with a cross on one side to mark the place where Our Lord was speared, high seaboots and a beaver hat. If he entered a cottage where he knew there was an unbaptised child he would sniff the air loudly and say: 'I smell brimstone.'

Susan Chitty
(b. 1929)

CHARLES KINGSLEY'S LANDSCAPE

He had strange allies. 'He is a holy man,' said the squire of ffrench's, Tory to the marrow, 'and I'll hear nothing against him.' The squire sometimes broke his village routine and treated himself to a morning service with Father N. He sat in the front row inhaling the incense and the ritual and finding it all vastly to his taste. Soon Father N. would mount the pulpit and the philippic would begin, perhaps that morning against vested interests and the private ownership of land. His words were anathema to the squire, or would have been if the squire had not been deaf. He heard nothing, he only knew that he was just below a holy man, and that was enough. Others knew what Father N. was likely to say and he had no illusions: 'They come to my church for the high jinks, just as they go to the Russian ballet.' But they knew that he meant and did what he said; that, just as he urged the rich to stop entertaining each other and to call in vagrants and give them a grand spread, so no vagrant went empty away from the vicarage. There would be a square meal inside him and perhaps a pair of boots and some old clothes in a bundle. The fact too that the speaker was a man of very old family sharpened his points, and affected the squire. Some may have found comfort in placing Father N. as another of the high-bred eccentrics that England throws up, another Cunninghame Graham, Scawen Blunt, or Mark Napier. 'Quite mad,' said a rector nearer home. But he could be strangely troubling to the mind. 'How he hates the rich,' whispered a woman who came with us to one of Father N.'s services at night, but she was wrong. He hated nobody. He recognized defeat, notably against the imperviousness of the smug. He would go for them, their complacency, their dullness and even the ugliness of their houses, and then pull up. 'Oh, well, God bless them,' he'd say in his mild way, and mean it. But if he hated many things of the world he loved and enjoyed many things of the earth, and on the short

Country People

way home to his house this fragile aristocrat, 'all patched up' as his garage friend called him and latterly very nearly blind, drank a pint of beer at the Bull. He died, and of all his obituaries the one that best fitted him was spoken by a man I was fetching to sweep our chimneys: 'He'll be greatly missed. I reckon he'd do 'most anything for anybody!'

Gerald Millar

Part-Time Countryman

Well connected, well-mannered and traditionally Tory, the Austens were qualified in every respect to be welcomed into the inner circle of this society, and all the more because Thomas Knight, chief landowner of the district, lived in Kent leaving [the Revd] George Austen as his representative to be consulted and deferred to as the acting squire. This did not involve them in any wild whirl of social activities but rather a steady leisurely spaced-out round of morning calls, dinner parties and card parties, varied now and again by some amateur music-making or an expedition to see a local beauty spot or a gathering at a neighbour's garden to eat strawberries or cherries as the season suggested. The gentlemen too, though not so far as we know George Austen, had much sporting life together, invited each other to shoot, met one another out hunting with the Vyne Pack.

David Cecil
(1902 - 1986)

A Portrait Of Jane Austen

The good old Vicar in this mansion dwelt
Plain as the flock dependent on his cares
For week-day comforts and for Sunday prayers,
He'd no spare wealth to follow fashion's whim
And if he had she'd little joys for him.
He kept no horse the hunting's sports to share,
He fed no dogs to run the harmless hare;
He'd nought to waste while hunger sought his shed,
And while he had it they ne'er wanted bread.
His chiefest pleasure charity possest
In having means to make another blest;
Little was his and little was required;
Could he do that 'twas all the wealth desired.
Tho' small the gift, 'twas given with greatest will,
And blessings o'er it made it greater still;
On want's sad tale he never closed his door,
He gave them something and he wished it more;
The beggar's heart, dismantled of its fears,
Leaped up and thanked him for his crust with tears.

John Clare
(1793 – 1864)

from *The Parish : Satyre*

... A vignette from local church history which I have found stimulating is of the origins of one of our churches. According to tradition the minister of the local church apprehended the village squire, a member of his church, in the act of buying and selling cattle on the Sabbath and chastised him vigorously. The squire, being a man of property and social standing, was somewhat put out by this rough treatment and responded with the words, 'Sir, that is no way to speak to a gentleman.' Undeterred the minister replied to the effect that he was not aware that he was speaking to a gentleman! The upshot of this verbal fracas was the expulsion of the minister from the church, who, nothing daunted, took a large part of the congregation with him and established a church on the other side of the river, which in turn established two daughter churches over the following generations.

Of course it would be foolish to recommend such a confrontational style to our contemporary ministry (although I suspect such ways are not dead). What is admirable is the sheer energy of the man and the congregation who, nothing daunted, simply pick up sticks and camp down elsewhere. It is not the sort of behaviour which endears itself to pastoral committees, yet it challenges a more circumspect age with its boldness.

Robin Pagan
(b.1943)
Reform Magazine
(November, 1988)

With the birth of her children Fanny abandoned the programme of cold water, hard work and simple food that Charles had laid down for her before their marriage, if she had ever adhered to it. For the rest of her life she was a devoted, perhaps too devoted, mother. She had longed for a baby ever since she herself was a child, wishing her dolls were made of flesh and blood and in her year of exile from Charles she had planned a 'Babe's Book', a collection of 'poetry, fairy tales and fables... for Ernest's edification' (it was always assumed that the first child would be a boy called Ernest). She was now determined that Rose and the children who might follow her should have only the best. She was never able to abandon the standards of her wealthy background and remains, to this day, 'a very grand lady' in the memory of her family. After the first autumn rains she decided that the rectory, which had seemed to her husband so 'neat and comfortable', was damp and unhealthy. 'It was an old house,' she wrote, 'that had not been repaired for more than a hundred years. It was damp and unwholesome, surrounded by ponds which overflowed with every heavy rain, and flooded, not only the garden and stables, but all the rooms on the ground floor, keeping up master and servants, sometimes all night, baling out the water in buckets.' She omitted to mention that these periodic innundations were a source of delight to Charles, at least in his younger days. 'Up to my knees in water,' he wrote exultantly 'working with a pick axe by candlelight to prevent all being washed away. But it all goes with me under the head of "fun". Something to do.'

Susan Chitty
(b.1929)

THE BEAST AND THE MONK

Irene Currie is the wife of the Pound Lane Baptist minister. She is thirty-nine and, unlike the other ministers' wives, was born and bred in the village. Before her marriage, she worked on the land.

'Our congregation has just died off like that, in a matter of months. It really gets you down. You see, our Chapel is the oldest one, and the majority of people who come here are the elderly and they haven't got families. And the young people that we did have, teenagers and so forth that we've brought up through Sunday school, well, once they become of age, all their friends go to High Street. They've got such a big crowd of people and it's only natural that our young people want to join them there. You can't do anything about it. So, you see, we're up against it here. But we struggle on with those that still want it. We thought of joining up with High Street, but it's out of the question, really. I know the row was over a hundred years ago with the other chapel, but people are funny. There's some who still say they would never cross the doors of High Street and so forth. So we must keep open. We still function. We get quite a lot of weddings and funerals, of course. It seems to be the main thing, funerals.

'So now I just visit the sick and answer the phone. My main work now, I suppose, is in the home. Your Church life really starts in the home, the way you bring your children up and their attitude towards things. Mind you, if I didn't have such a big place here, and if it wasn't such a hole, I should love to get out. For my mental attitude as much as anything. I would, really. I don't come in contact with much here. I'm just here, in this corner, this hole.'

Mary Chamberlain
(b.1947)

Fen Women

LAY OFFICERS AND PREACHERS

Sometimes we meet the minister and his man in other circumstances. The story goes that when a certain University sold her honours, a minister, who deemed that his ministrations would be more acceptable and more useful if he possessed a doctorate, put £15 in his purse, and went to that university to purchase for himself a degree. His man-servant accompanied him, and was present when his master was formally admitted to the long-desired honour. On his return, "the Doctor" addressed his servant somewhat as follows, "Noo, Saunders, ye'll aye be sure to ca' me the Doctor; and gin onybody spiers at you aboot me, ye' li be aye sure to say, 'the Doctor's in his study,' or 'the Doctor's engaged,' or, 'the Doctor will see you in a crack.' "That a' depends," was the reply, "on whether you ca' me the Doctor, too." The Reverend Doctor stared. "Ay, it's juist so," continued the beadle, "for when I fand that it cost sae little, I e'en got a diploma mysel'. Sae ye'll juist be guid eneuch to say 'Doctor, 'put on some coals,' or 'Doctor, bring the whisky and hot water;' and gin onybody spiers at ye aboot me, ye'll be sure to say, 'the Doctor's in the pantry,' or 'the Doctor's diggin' potatoes,' as the case may be."

William Harvey
(1874 – 1936)

SCOTTISH LIFE AND CHARACTER

Tom Linnell was the most popular man not only in the village, but in the whole district. Born soon after Waterloo, he belonged to an older generation than mine. Close on six feet, beautifully built, one of the handsomest men I have ever seen, and possessed of a ready wit, he could not long have remained hid in any society, and, had Destiny decreed that he should appear on a larger stage, he must have become a celebrity. A famous local cricketer and quoit-player, a keen follower of the Grafton, champion swordsman of the Bucks Hussars, bandmaster, choirmaster, Sunday School teacher, and at times churchwarden, he sustained so many parts in the life of the parish and neighbourhood that it was often difficult to be sure what he was and what he was not at any moment.

It goes without saying that a man of his type would be a churchman and a Blue, and indeed he was one of the strongest pillars Church and State ever had in Silson. As churchwarden he was quite an autocrat. For a parson he could respect he would do anything in his power.

J. E. Linnell
(1842 – 1919)

OLD OAK

'It is a difficult matter to decide which is looked upon as the greatest man in a country church, the parson or his clerk,' wrote Cowper. 'The latter is most certainly held in higher veneration, where the former happens to be only a poor curate, who rides every Sabbath from village to village, and mounts and dismounts at the church door. The clerk's office is not only to tag the prayers with an Amen, or usher in the sermon with a stave; but he is also the universal father to give away the brides, and the standing godfather to all the newborn bantlings.' The poet summed up the situation in a deft couplet:

> There goes the parson, oh! illustrious spark,
> And there, scarce less illustrious, goes the clerk.

The duties of this great man also included the recording of births, the keeping of the church accounts, the washing of surplices and the waking of those who slumbered during service. The so-called 'sluggard-waker' used a long staff with a heavy knob attached, with which to rap the dozing men and beat the mischievous children. He also had a fox's brush, for politely stirring the sleeping females. The squire of Kinver in Staffordshire offered Thomas, the clerk, five shillings to wake any elder or farmer who slept, however rich or important the man might be. Thomas did as he was told and brought his staff down on the squire's own head. He then held out his hand for the five-shilling reward.

Simon Goodenough
(b.1945)

The Country Parson

The backbone of Wellington's army in Spain was reputed to be its sergeants, and we can say with just as much truth that the backbone of Methodism in its early days was its local preachers. Very different were they from their modern-day successors with their kid gloves, patent-leather boots and the semi-clerical attire so many of them affect. For the greater part they were men as rugged in speech as in appearance. Some, like old Lovell, had been fighting men or wrestlers; others, as small farmers or farm labourers, had been brought up on the land, and in many cases their "Sunday Best" was a smock frock. But they were men with convictions; they spoke in language "understanded of the people", and as a rule, their preaching was backed up by their consistent lives.

Long before my day an old farmer who often preached at Silson was able to overcome the prejudices of even such valiants for the Church as Edward and his sons. Not a more bigoted churchwoman ever lived than my grandmother; yet more than once she was heard to express her admiration for old Master Bennett and to say that, if ever she should enter a chapel – though it was not likely she would – it would be to hear him. Fragments of his sermons were still preserved in the memories of old people when I was a boy. That he did not spare his co-religionists when he thought they needed rebuke is very evident. This is a scrap of one of his addresses: "Some o' you folk are tryin' to shift your sins from your own souls to the devil's shoulders, and he, like a pa-atient pack-horse, stands ready to receive 'em. If you are convicted o' doin' wrong, you say, 'That wur the devil – that wur the devil!' I say, 'twarn't the devil; 'twur yourself as sinned, an', if this be the way you think you be a-gooin' to esca-ape' the consequences o' your wrong-doin's, you'll find by an' by that he has an ahkud knack of returnin' what has never bin hisn, but your own from fust to last!"

M.K. Ashby

Joseph Ashby of Tysoe

As a consequence the only communal relaxations for the crofters within the village were the church services on Sundays; the biannual communions; an election meeting once in five years and an even less frequent lecture by the poultry adviser, more familiarly known as the 'henwife'. During the winter months our evenings were sometimes enlivened by the visits of young lay preachers, locally termed 'pilgrims', who, with varying degrees of fanaticism, would exhort us poor sinners – who listened with varying degrees of perplexity – to forsake our evil ways and return to the paths of righteousness. Some of the pilgrims stayed for as long as a week amongst us and every night we would endure the hard benches of the church while they, with white strained faces, tear-filled eyes and voices that not only grated with emotion but also implied chronic deafness of the congregation if not of the Almighty, besought for us forgiveness and salvation. Mouthing the name of the Deity with expletive violence they would adjure us to give up our pipe-smoking, our church socials and our concubines. (Curiously enough I never heard alcoholism specifically mentioned as a sin but I suppose even the most zealous of pilgrims must recognize the hopelessness of some tasks.)

'What's a concubine?' Erchy asked, after one such meeting.

'It's a woman a man takes to live with him but who isn't his wife,' I explained.

'A mistress, like?'

'Yes.'

'Indeed we don't do that sort of thing hereabouts,' refuted Erchy. 'Why would we take them to live with us when they have homes of their own already?'

But, at a ceilidh a few weeks later at Morag's house, Erchy referred again to the subject of concubinage.

'I didn't think when those pilgrims was here that I knew of anybody hereabouts that was livin' with a woman who wasn't his wife, but I remembered afterwards about Dodo.'

'He's no from Bruach,' someone contradicted.

'No, I know fine he's not, but he was livin' with a woman, right enough. And what's more he's had three children by her.'

'That fellow!' ejaculated Morag with righteous scorn.

Dodo was a shiftless, happy-go-lucky, slow-witted character who lived in a nearby village. His house was patchily cement-washed and his croft work was never quite finished because he was for ever neglecting it to start on some new job which in its turn was dropped before completion because some other project had taken his fancy. 'Well,' went on Erchy, 'when the pilgrims left here they went on to Dodo's place and they must have got a good hold of Dodo for I'm hearin' now that he and that woman slipped off quietly to Glasgow and he's married her.'

'Married her? After all these years?' we all echoed incredulously.

'Aye, that's what I'm hearin' and I believe it's the truth.'

There was a moment of silence as everyone digested the news and then Morag said, philosophically: 'Well, if he has, it's the first time I've ever known that man finish a job once he'd begun it.'

Lillian Beckwith
(b.1916)

THE SEA FOR BREAKFAST

CHURCH MUSICIANS AND BELL RINGERS

'Well,' said Timothy Fairway, feeling demands upon his praise in some form or other, ''tis a worthy thing to be married, Mr Wildeve; and the woman you've got is a dimant, so says I. Yes,' he continued, to Grandfer Cantle, raising his voice so as to be heard through the partition; 'her father (inclining his head towards the inner room) was as good a feller as ever lived. He always had his great indignation ready against anything underhand.'

'Is that very dangerous?' said Christian.

'And there were few in these parts that were upsides with him.' said Sam. 'Whenever a club walked he'd play the clarinet in the band that marched before 'em as if he'd never touched anything but a clarinet all his life. And then, when they got to church-door he'd throw down the clarinet, mount the gallery, snatch up the bass-viol, and rozum away as if he'd never played anything but a bass-viol. Folk would say – folk that knowed what a true stave was – "Surely, surely that's never the same man that I saw handling the clarinet so masterly by now!"'

'I can mind it,' said the furze-cutter. ''Twas a wonderful thing that one body could hold it all and never mix the fingering.'

'There was Kingsbere church likewise,' Fairway recommenced, as one opening a new vein of the same mine of interest.

Wildeve breathed the breath of one intolerably bored, and glanced through the partition at the prisoners.

'He used to walk over there of a Sunday afternoon to visit his old acquaintance Andrew Brown, the first clarinet there; a good man enough, but rather screechy in his music, if you can mind?'

'"A was.'

'And neighbour Yeobright would take Andrey's place for some part of the service, to let Andrey have a bit of a nap, as any friend would naturally do.'

'As any friend would,' said Grandfer Cantle, the other listeners expressing the same accord by the shorter way of nodding their heads.

'No sooner was Andrey asleep and the first whiff of neighbour Yeobright's wind had got inside Andrey's clarinet than every one in church felt in a moment there was a great soul among 'em. All heads would turn, and they'd say, "Ah, I thought 'twas he!" One Sunday I can well mind – a bass-viol day that time, and Yeobright had brought his own. 'Twas the Hundred-and-thirty-third to "Lydia"; and when they'd come to "Ran down his beard and o'er his robes its costly moisture shed", neighbour Yeobright, who had just warmed to his work, drove his bow into them strings that glorious grand that he e'en a'most sawed the bass-viol into two pieces. Every winder in church rattled as if 'twere a thunderstorm. Old Pa'son Williams lifted his hands on his great holy surplice as natural as if he'd been in common clothes, and seemed to say to hisself, "O for such a man in our parish!" But not a soul in Kingsbere could hold a candle to Yeobright.'

Thomas Hardy
(1840 – 1928)

RETURN OF THE NATIVE

A holiday in a small village on the North Devon Coast provided me with yet another fascinating experience of singing in a church choir other than my own.

The vicar, who said that if I really wanted to sing in the choir I was very welcome – and made it sound like a desperate warning – took me along to the church before Evensong to show me some of its finer features …

On the pretence that he saw a parishioner approaching, the vicar now directed me to a moth-eaten green baize door, and dissolved into the shadows. I forged ahead alone and entered the choir vestry.

It was so dim in here that I thought I was one of those pilgrims who keep on marching through the night of doubt and sorrow …

In the great tradition of church choirs everyone suddenly materialized about two minutes before the service was due to start. But these were experts. They were ready, men, boys and girls, dead on time …

We were accommodated round the organ in a gallery at the back of the church, so while the vicar entered the chancel dignified and alone, the choir clambered to their places up a ladder and through a trapdoor. When the hollow clumping of hobnailed boots and clatter of high heels had subsided, the vicar cast one apprehensive and despairing glance at the gallery to make sure that we were unfortunately all there, and then took no more notice of us.

I think he was trying to forget us, because he seemed to address himself entirely to the Colonel who sat with his party in the front pew. And it was quite obvious that the Colonel, despite his eighty years, was very much in charge.

For instance, this was the only church I had discovered where the congregation led the choir in the singing. As soon as a hymn was announced the Colonel would lead off his supporters with a melodious parade-ground bellow which put them well ahead of the choir, who were still finding their places. Then the organist would desperately try to overtake the choir, who would never wait for him in the futile efforts to draw level with the congregation.

To a stranger all this was a little disconcerting, but if you thought of the hymns as three part rounds it wasn't at all bad, and the Amens were really fascinating with their unique alpine echo effect.

The Evensong included a community hymn singing session, so we had many opportunities to beat the Colonel, but we never did. Always we arrived at the last verse a breathlessly gallant second, with the organist a bad third.

Of course the inference mght be drawn that the parties concerned could not have been on very good terms, but this would be quite wrong. The Colonel had been a great sportsman in his day and had always appreciated worthy, game opponents.

Reginald Frary
(b.1920)

Don't Upset the Choir

'Good evening, good evening! This is good of you. Anyone in sight? No sense of time, these people! Nearly half past now! Enough to drive you mad!' His words jerked out as he darted breathlessly about. A leaflet fluttered down to the hideous lozenge-patterned carpet which covers the chancel floor.

As he was scrabbling it up wildly, we heard the sound of country voices at the door, and a little knot of people entered. Mr Willet and his wife were there, two or three of my older pupils, looking sheepish at seeing me in an unusual setting, and Mrs Pringle brought up the rear. Mrs Pringle's booming contralto voice tends to drown the rest of the choir with its peculiarly strong carrying qualities. As her note reading is far from accurate, and she resents any sort of correction, Mrs. Pringle is rather more of a liability than an asset to St Patrick's church choir; but her aggressive piety, expressing itself in the deepest genuflections, the most military sharp-turns to the east and the raising of eyes to the chancel roof, is an example to the fidgety choir-boys, and Mr Annett bears with her mannerisms with commendable fortitude.

I went through to the vestry to see if Eric, my organ blower, was at his post. The vestry was warm and homely. The table was covered with a red serge cloth with a fringe of bobbles. On it stood a massive ink bottle containing an inch of ink, which had dried to the consistency of honey. Leaning negligently against the table was Eric, looking unpleasantly grubby, and blowing gum bubbles from his mouth in a placid way.

'It don't hurt you,' Eric reassured me. 'I often eats it – gives you the hiccups sometimes. That's all.'

Shaken, I returned to the organ and set out the music. Four or five more choir members had arrived and Mr. Annett was fidgeting to begin. Snatches of conversation drifted over to me.

'But a guinea, mark you, just for killing an old pig!'

'Ah! But you got all the meat and lard and that, look! I knows you has to keep 'um all the year, and a guinea do seem a lot, I'll own up, but still –'

'Well, well!' broke in Mr Annett's staccato voice. 'Shall we make a start?'

'Young Mrs Pickett said to tell you she'd be along presently when she'd got the baby down. He's been a bit poorly –'

This piece of news started a fresh burst of comment, while Mr Annett raised and lowered himself impatiently on his toes.

'Poor little crow! Teeth, I don't wonder!'

'She called in nurse.'

'Funny, that! I see her only this morning up the shop – '

Mr Annett's patience snapped suddenly. He rattled his baton on the reading desk and flashed his eyes.

'Please, please! I'm afraid we must begin without Mrs Pickett. Ready, Miss Read? One, two!' We were off.

Behind me the voices rose and fell, Mrs Pringle's concentrated lowing vying with Mrs. Willet's nasal soprano. Mrs Willet clings to her notes so cloyingly that she is usually half a bar behind the rest. Her voice has that penetrating and lugubrious quality found in female singers' renderings of 'Abide With Me' outside public houses on Saturday nights. She has a tendency to over-emphasize the final consonants and draw out the vowels to such excruciating lengths, and all this executed with such devilish shrillness, that every nerve is set jangling.

This evening Mrs. Willet's time-lag was even worse than usual. Mr Annett called a halt.

'This,' he pleaded, 'is a cheerful lively piece of music. The valleys, we're told, laugh and sing. Lightly, please, let it trip, let it be merry! Miss Read, could you play it again?'

As trippingly and as nimbly as I could I obliged, watching Mr Annett's black, nodding head in the mirror above the organ. The tuft of his double crown flicked half a beat behind the rest of his head.

'Once more!' he commanded, and obediently the heavy, measured tones dragged forth, Mr Annett's baton beating a brisk but independent rhythm. Suddenly he flung his hands up and gave a slight scream. The choir slowed to a ragged halt and pained glances were exchanged. Mrs Pringle's mouth was buttoned into its most disapproving lines, and even Mrs Willet's stolid countenance was faintly perturbed.

'The time! The time!' shouted Mr Annett, baton pounding on the desk. 'Listen again!' He gesticulated menacingly at my mirror and I played it again. 'You hear it? It goes:

'They dance, bong-bong,

They sing, bong-bong,

They dance, BONG and BONG, sing BONG-BONG!

It's just as simple as that! Now, with me!"

With his hair on end and his eyes gleaming dangerously, Mr Annett led them once more into action. Gallantly they battled on, Mr Annett straining like an eager puppy at the leash, while the slow voices rolled steadily along behind.

Miss Read

(b.1913)

Village School

The week before Christmas, when snow seemed to lie thickest, was the moment for carol-singing; and when I think back to those nights it is to the crunch of snow and to the lights of the lanterns on it. Carol-singing in my village was a special tithe for the boys, the girls had little to do with it. Like hay-making, blackberrying, stone-clearing, and wishing-people-a-happy-Easter, it was one of our seasonal perks.

By instinct we knew just when to begin; a day too soon and we should have been unwelcome, a day too late and we should have received lean looks from people whose bounty was already exhausted. When the true moment came, exactly balanced, we recognized it and were ready.

So as soon as the wood had been stacked in the oven to dry for the morning fire, we put on our scarves and went out through the streets, calling loudly between our hands, till the various boys who knew the signal ran out from their houses to join us.

One by one they came stumbling over the snow, swinging their lanterns around their heads, shouting and coughing horribly.

'Come carol-barking then?'

We were the Church Choir, so no answer was necessary. For a year we had praised the Lord out of key, and as a reward for this service – on top of the Outing – we now had the right to visit all the big houses, to sing our carols and collect our tribute.

To work them all in meant a five-mile foot journey over wild and generally snowed-up country. So the first thing we did was to plan our route; a formality, as the route never changed. All the same, we blew on our fingers and argued; and then we chose our Leader. This was not binding, for we all fancied ourselves as Leaders, and he who started the night in that position usually trailed home with a bloody nose.

Eight of us set out that night. There was sixpence the Tanner, who had never sung in his life (he just worked his mouth in church); the brothers Horace and Boney, who were always fighting everybody and always getting the worst of it; Clergy Green, the preaching maniac; Walt the bully, and my two brothers. As we went down the lane other boys, from other villages, were already about the hills, bawling 'Kingwenslush', and shouting through keyholes 'Knock on the knocker! Ring the Bell! Give us a penny for singing so well!' They weren't an approved charity as we were, the Choir; but competition was in the air.

Our first call as usual was the house of the Squire, and we trouped nervously down his drive. For light we had candles in marmalade-jars suspended on loops of string, and they threw pale gleams on the towering snowdrifts that stood on each side of the drive. A blizzard was blowing, but we were well wrapped up, with Army puttees on our legs, woollen hats on our heads, and several scarves around our ears.

As we approached the Big House across its white silent lawns, we too grew respectfully silent. The lake near by was stiff and black, the waterfall frozen and still. We arranged ourselves shuffling around the big front door, then knocked and announced the Choir.

A maid bore the tidings of our arrival away into the echoing distances of the house, and while we waited we cleared our throats noisily. Then she came back, and the door was left ajar for us, and we were bidden to begin. We brought no music, the carols were in our heads. 'Let's give 'em "Wild Shepherds",' said Jack. We began in confusion, plunging into a wreckage of keys, of different words and tempo; but we gathered our strength; he who sang loudest took the rest of us with him, and the carol took shape if not sweetness.

This huge stone house, with its ivied walls, was always a mystery to us. What were those gables, those rooms and attics, those narrow windows veiled by the cedar trees. As we sang 'Wild Shepherds' we craned our necks, gaping into that lamplit hall which we had never entered; staring at the muskets and untenanted chairs, the great tapestries furred by dust until suddenly, on the stairs, we saw the old Squire himself standing and listening with his head on one side.

He didn't move until we'd finished; then slowly he tottered towards us, dropped two coins in our box with a trembling hand, scratched his name in the book we carried, gave us each a long look with his moist blind eyes, then turned away in silence.

As though released from a spell, we took a few sedate steps, then broke into a run for the gate. We didn't stop till we were out of the grounds. Impatient, at last, to discover the extent of his bounty, we squatted by the cowsheds, held our lanterns over the book, and saw he had written 'Two Shillings'. This was quite a good start. No one of any worth in the district would dare to give us less than the Squire.

Laurie Lee
(1914 – 1986)

CIDER WITH ROSIE

She hung up her stocking at the foot of the bed and fell asleep. But soon singing roused her, and she sat up, bewildered. Yes, it was the carol-singers.

Margaret came running upstairs and wrapped her in a blanket. She took her across the landing to her own room, and pulled up the linen blind.

Outside under the stars she could see the group of men and women with lanterns throwing beams across the paths and on to the stable door. One man stood apart beating time, another played a fiddle, and another had a flute. The rest sang in four parts the Christmas hymns, "While shepherds watched", "Come all ye faithful", and "Hark, the herald angels sing".

There was the star, Susan could see it twinkling and bright in the dark boughs with their white frosted layers, and there was the stable. She watched the faces half lit by the lanterns, top-coats pulled up to their necks. The music of the violin came thin and squeaky, like a singing icicle, blue and cold, but magic, and the flute was warm like the voices.

They stopped and waited a moment. Tom's deep voice came from the darkness. They trooped, chattering and puffing out their cheeks, and clapping their arms round their bodies, to the front door. They were going to the parlour for elderberry wine and their collection of money. A bright light flickered across the snow as the door was flung wide open. Then a bang, and Susan went back to bed.

Alison Uttley
(1889 – 1976)

COUNTRY WORLD

Hilary hastened down the church and caught Jack Godfrey up just as he emerged from the winding stair into the ringing chamber.

'I've come to watch you do the bells, Mr. Godfrey. Shall I be in your way?'

'Why, no, Miss Hilary, I'd be very pleased for you to come. You better go first up them ladders, same as I can help you if you was to slip.'

'I shan't slip.' said Hilary scornfully. She climbed briskly up the thick and ancient rungs, to emerge into the chamber which formed the second story of the tower ...

Jack Godfrey followed her up soberly, carrying his grease and cleaning-rags.

'Be a bit careful of the floor, Miss Hilary,' he urged, 'it's none so good in places...'

The trap-door that led to the bell-chamber was shut; a chain ran down from it, vanishing into a sort of wooden case upon the wall. Godfrey produced a key from his bunch and unlocked this case, disclosing the counterpoise. He pulled it down and the trap swung open.

'Why is that kept locked, Mr. Godfrey?'

'Well, Miss Hilary, now and again it has happened as the ringers has left the belfry door open, and Rector says it ain't safe. You see, that Potty Peake might come a-traipsing round, or some of they mischeevious lads might come up here and get larking about with the bells. Or they might go up the tower and fall off and hurt theirselves. So Rector said to fix a lock the way they couldn't get the trap-door open.'

'I see.' Hilary grinned a little. 'Hurt theirselves' was a moderate way of expressing the probable result of a hundred-and-twenty-foot fall. She led the way up the second ladder.

By contrast with the brilliance below, the bell-chamber was sombre and almost menacing...

The bells, with mute black mouths gaping downwards, brooded in their ancient places.

Mr. Godfrey, eyeing them with the cheerful familiarity born of long use, fetched a light ladder that stood against the wall, set it up carefully against one of the cross-beams, and prepared to mount.

'Let me go up first, or I shan't see what you're doing.'

Mr Godfrey paused and scratched his head. The proposal did not seem quite safe to him. He voiced an objection.

'I shall be quite all right; I can sit on the beam. I don't mind heights one bit. I'm very good at gym.'

Sir Henry's daughter was accustomed to have her own way, and got it – with the stipulation that she should hold on very tightly by the timber of the cage and not let go or "morris about". The promise being given, she was assisted to her lofty perch. Mr. Godfrey, whistling a lively air between his teeth, arranged his materials methodically about him and proceeded with his task, greasing the gudgeons and trunnions, administering a spot of oil to the pulley-axle, testing the movement of the slider between the blocks and examining the rope for signs of friction where it passed over wheel and pulley.

'I've never seen Tailor Paul as close as this before. She's a big bell, isn't she?'

'Pretty fair,' said Jack Godfrey, approvingly, giving the bell a friendly pat on her bronze shoulder...

'Many a good ring have we had out of her, not to say a sight of funerals and passing-bells. And we rung her with Gaude for them there Zeppelin raids, to give the alarm like…'

Gaude, Sabaoth, John, Jericho, Jubilee, and Dimity each in her turn was visited and anointed. When, however, it came to the turn of Batty Thomas, Mr. Godfrey displayed a sudden and unexpected obstinacy.

'I'm not taking you up to Batty Thomas, Miss Hilary. She's an unlucky bell. What I mean, she's a bell that has her fancies and I wouldn't like for to risk it.'

'What do you mean?'

Mr. Godfrey found it difficult to express himself more plainly.

'She's my own bell,' he said; 'I've rung her close on fifteen year now and I've looked after her for ten, ever since Hezekiah got too old for these here ladders. Her and me knows one another and she've no quarrel with me nor I with her. But she's queer-tempered. They do say as how old Batty down below, what had her put up here, was a queer sort of man and his bell's took after him. When they turned out the monks and that — a great many years ago, that'd be — they do say as Batty Thomas tolled a whole night through on her own like, without a hand laid to the rope. And when Cromwell sent his men to break up the images an' that, there was a soldier come up here into the belfry, I don't know for what, maybe to damage the bells, but anyhow, up he come; and some of the others, not knowing he was here, began to haul on the ropes, and it seems as how the bells must have been left mouth up. Careless ringers they must have been in those days, but anyhow, that's how 'twas. And just as this soldier was leaning over to look at the bells, like, Batty Thomas came singing down and killed him dead. That's history, that is, and Rector says as how Batty Thomas saved the church, because the soldiers took fright and ran away, thinking it was a judgment, though to my thinking, it was just carelessness, leaving the bell that fashion. Still, there it was. And then, there was a poor lad in old Rector's time learning to ring, and he tried to raise Batty Thomas and got hisself hanged in the rope. A terrible thing that was, and there again, I say it was carelessness and the lad didn't ought to have been let practice all alone, and it's a thing Mr. Venables never will allow. But you see, Miss Hilary, Batty Thomas has killed two men, and while it's quite understandable as there was carelessness both times or it wouldn't have happened – well! I wouldn't like to take any risks, like I said.'

And with this as his last word on the subject, Mr. Godfrey mounted aloft to grease the gudgeons of Batty Thomas unassisted.

Dorothy L. Sayers
(1893 – 1957)

THE NINE TAYLORS

Ashton bellringers, all five of them, looked thoughtfully at the dying embers in the schoolroom grate. This was the very last supper for them in the century. The village women had cleared and washed up the crocks, Dr. Overthrow, who had been chairman once more, had gone home to sit the old year out and the new year in.

'Another hour and it ull be nineteen hundred,' said John Stallard, Captain of Ashton's Church Tower.

'Oi and the old Queen's still on the throne,' spoke up young Jim Bowman. 'Good 'ooman her a bin, our old man rung the treble bell, same as I does, at the Coronation.'

The nine-gallon barrel, trammed and tapped in the corner of the schoolroom, just dribbled another mugful for Jim Bowman's brother, George.

'He's a getting low,' Joe Bradfield belched, 'like the year, oi and the century – almost gone. Pack a feow writing slates a' the backside on him, I can do with another pint; 'tis like the tay pot – some a the best's in the bottom,' and with this Frank Wheatcroft helped Joe to tilt the barrel. Nothing stirred in Ashton School after the last dregs had been drained from the barrel; there was just the monotonous tick tick of the clock, the wheeze of pipe lighting as a pall of blue tobacco smoke rose to the rafters.

Then John Stallard spoke, 'Now then, you chaps, look lissom, it only wants twenty-five minutes to twelve.' As the men rose to walk down the road to the church the chill night air penetrated their thick cord trousers. Soon they were in the belfry. By lantern light, like their fathers before them, five men stood in a little circle. At John's signal the sally end of the rope was grasped and away went the team. One, two, three, four, five. A merry peal, the last merry peal of the nineteenth century. Nods from John again at ten to twelve; ringing stopped while up among the woodwork and the furrowed wheels where ropes had worn themselves out time and time again, the bells stood green and cold.

'Look slippy, Jim, we an't got all night, bring up the leather mufflers.'

These were fixed in position to muffle the sound of the bells as the old year departed. 'Mufflers in position,' John reported. 'Now for the Buff Peal as we calls it. Mind they be only half muffled.'

The ringing began again, ding, dong, ding, dong, ding. Balm, Balm, Balm, Balm, Balm, the death of the year and the century.

'It's sad mind, five more minutes according to the clock in the ringing chamber,' John shouted above the noise of the bells.

Jim Bowman's thoughts wandered to his father ringing for the Queen's Coronation and how the five Ashton men had rung for two Jubilees. The Queen could not live much longer. Then another Coronation, a king this time. The minutes ticked by until twelve when that pause the villagers waited for arrived.

'Happy New Year,' John said for one and all, ' and let's have them mufflers off. Now for some ringing, you chaps.'

George grabbed his sally. 'Pity we a only got five bells, if we had six we ud ring a peal to be sure.'

'Fire um!' ordered John, and like one man five ringers pulled together and all the bells rang out over the countryside like cannon in battle. 'Keep firing um, we shan't see the end a the nineteen hundreds.'

Fred Archer
(b.1915)

THE SECRETS OF BREDON HILL

CHURCH COUNCILS AND CHURCHGOERS

'It would be nice,' said Mrs Turner, 'if we could have a new flag.' Then she sped out of the room. In that huge billowing dress, she made me think of a galleon – sailing under a new flag, perhaps.

It had been one of those church council meetings when everyone found something on which to spend our income, but no one could think of any novel means by which the income might be increased.

Geoff Wainwright had suggested a sponsored walk, only to meet with a chorus of 'What, in this weather?' Shy young Alison Metcalf, with the long blond hair and a lisp, had whispered, 'We could always have another beetle drive.'

'No, there was too much cheatin' at t'last one!' That was the verdict of Elsie Martin, and as such, it was uncontestable. Elsie was, well, an even grander lady than Emily Turner, and her opinion had not been challenged since the end of the last war...

So, we were to rely on the usual garden party, on the winter series of whist drives and on my annual letter in the church magazine, asking for an increase in contributions to the planned giving scheme.

The flag in question was the Union Jack which draped the war memorial on the south wall of the nave. It had seen many campaigns against the moths and there were more holes in it than if it had seen live action. Emily Turner's concern for our flag was well known. She was the one who took it down every year at the beginning of Lent and washed it. She had begun that church meeting by warning us all, 'I daren't put it in the washer. It looks as if it'll come apart in my hands.' By way of demonstrating the tendency of fabric to corruption, she seized a pleat of voluminous dress and rubbed it between her fingers.

'Aye, well. There are other things need attending to before we start chucking money about on old flags,' said Arnold Davies.

He might as well have uttered the prince of heresies. Emily's eyes flashed. 'What other things?'

The question was loaded, because she knew very well what Arnold would like to spend some of the church's money on, if he got the chance. He was a keen member of the choir and he had been, for a long time, wanting to buy a new set of Merbecke's music for the Holy Communion.

The sparse conversation seemed to proceed telepathically. Arnold said nothing more, but the fact that he had spoken at all led Emily to continue, 'In my day we used to have Communion said, without music. And a lot of us thought it was a lot more holier.'

Church council meetings often proceed on the principle of digression: talk about the flag led to a debate on the music used at the main service, and that ended up as a discussion about whether the organist's honorarium ought to be increased.

That was where Arnold Davies came in again. 'I told you there were other things we should spend our money on.'

'Could, not should, Mr Davies. We used to make do without an organist at the morning service…', she added the words, 'in my day', as if referring to some distant, unrecoverable golden age.

In the end, we decided nothing about either the organist's honorarium or the flag, except that Alec Ridsdale suggested Mrs. Turner should be asked to discover all she could about costs and bring the information to the next meeting. There being no further business, the meeting closed at 9.45 pm and most of the members adjourned to The Acorn for the last half-hour.

Peter Mullen
(b.1942)

COUNTRY MATTERS

The first thing that struck me on entering the south porch was a board conspicuously hung up, on which were the words – 'TAKE OFF YOUR PATTENS,' painted in plain letters, a very necessary injunction in a rural parish, considering the dreadful clatter the iron-shod damsels sometimes make.

All the natives looked at me, but nobody offered me a seat, so I helped myself to the first I saw, and which I occupied in conjunction with an old ploughman and a boy in an ambitious livery coat. A stranger in a retired rural church, especially if he happen to wear spectacles and broadcloth, is an event too remarkable in the annals of the parish to be lightly overlooked, and my friends around me stared at the new comer as if they would have said, "I wonder who you are, and where you come from, and what brings you here." A man who was standing at the intersections of the transepts, nave, and chancel, and pulling away at the bell-rope, presenting rather a prominent figure in the scene, appeared indeed as if he would almost ask the question; even the school children, who, headed by the master carrying a music-book in his hand, entered in long file through the south door of the chancel, and who came pat, pat, clatter in their wooden shoes up the aisle, immediately descried the stranger, and looked over their snub noses at me as if I had two heads. Well, thought I, it would seem as if Yatton was not often favoured with the visits of an illustrious stranger; I must get out of the way as soon as possible after the service, lest the church-wardens be for waiting on me with a deputation to present an address.

As soon as the clergyman entered the reading-desk, however, the people turned their eyes from me to their prayer books.

There is an old joke of an Oxford spark saying he would give any man the Creed and beat him before he came to the end of the Litany. I really believe from the rate at which he read, that the incumbent of Yatton might do this with ease: I attempted to keep up with him, but finding the pace impossible I closed my book, and listened with resignation …

While I am in my captious mood I shall endeavour to dispose of all my fault-finding at once: I would, therefore, recommend the minister to rebuke his flock for a practice, which they have in common with most rural congregations, namely of turning their backs to the clergyman when the Te Deum and Jubilate are being performed and the psalms sung, leaning deliberately on their elbows, and looking up at the organ-loft as if they were listening to the music in front of a fair booth, instead of 'singing to the praise and glory of God'. The organ was a large, and for a country church, an elaborate instrument. It was once surmounted by three allegorical and musical figures, comprising King David, with gilt harp strings and knee buckles, and two Vicars Choral of Honduras mahogany, whom he is in the act of accompanying; but these have of late, like Darius, 'fallen from their high estate,' and occupy lower posts full in front of the gallery.

The text was a short and comprehensive one – 'The wages of sin is death.' The same fault that I find with him in the reading-desk applied to the preacher's manner in the pulpit. His delivery was rapid, irregular, and unequal; and, owing to these causes nothing, but the most careful attention could enable me to comprehend a sermon which was in itself simple, solemn, and unaffected: preached with more deliberation the discourse would have been everything one could wish – a good plain country-church sermon, suited to the education and condition of his audience.

Joseph Leech
(1815 – 1893)

RURAL RIDES OF THE BRISTOL CHURCHGOER

Hill Christmas

They came over the snow to the bread's
purer snow, fumbled it in their huge hands,
put their lips to it like beasts, stared into the dark chalice
where the wine shone, felt it sharp
on their tongue, shivered as at a sin
remembered, and heard love cry
momentarily in their hearts' manger.
They rose and went back to their poor
holdings, naked in the bleak light
of December. Their horizon contracted
to one small, stone-riddled field
with its tree, where the weather was nailing
the appalled body that had asked to be born.

R.S.Thomas
(b.1913)

Nelly, sitting at the back, could see the whole village in front of her. The farmers sat in their family pews, even old Hartley Procter, who still came to play cards with her Dad. A right pair of old gamecocks, the two of them. She could see Hartley Procter's shirt collar sticking up even in that dim light, as if it showed his resentment at having to wear a tie. Billy-a-Doad, his head nodding just above the pew back, sat beside the aisle, his married sons and their families filling two pews entirely. William Edmonson and his wife, a weatherbeaten, upright pair, sat at the front.

The quarrymen were scattered down the sides, bunched close to heating grilles in the floor. There were lads she had been at school with sitting among their children. Frank Brown, still quarry engineer, sat alone, his little, dirty, old mother long dead, and his rough brother, John James, was also dead, killed by a stroke one hot day in the quarry. Nelly thought of John James and his stubborn system of organ blowing. 'John James ... James, you're going too fast,' would come a desperate whisper from the organist, and in the deep silence, as everyone took breath for the next line, John James' reply echoed round the church, 'I'm blowing for "God save the Queen", tha can play what tha likes.' Now Reuben pumped the organ. He was more biddable.

Roger Mason
(b. 1940)

Granny's Village

Most children and all adults were members of one of three churches.

C. of E's would have been christened and confirmed at Ashdon or Bartlow Church, both two miles away from our house. But because our Bartlow Hamlet was not like an ordinary

End of Ashdon, we could go to either village church. But we had to steer clear of the village chapel, whose Baptists had been initiated or made members, sometimes at the ripe age of seventy years, by the wet and- perishing public process of total immersion in 'that owd sheep-dip', wherein many gallons of holy water stagnated beneath the rostrum of the chapel. Thus we had three preparatory schools for Paradise, whose parsons did their best to lure sheep from other flocks by cottage visits, flattery and cajolery. And Lord have mercy on the soul of one who switched from church to chapel – or vice versa, for the villagers would never forgive a 'Devil-dodger'.

Granny Ford was not a Devil-dodger. Because she had been christened at Bartlow Church she would not attend another except for Harvest Festival. She had been christened, confirmed, married, and would be buried at Bartlow, as would several of her children. For fifty years she had walked over two miles back and forth to Bartlow Church each Friday to clean, dust, scrub and polish it. This took all day and was done solely for love. She had not missed one Friday in those fifty years.

Also, once a fortnight Grandfather Ford would walk there and back for equally selfless reasons – tools over bent shoulders to tidy verges, rake grass and paths and put in trim untidy, neglected graves.

Spike Mays
(b.1907)

REUBEN'S CORNER

CHAPTER 4

WORK

ALL SORTS OF WORK

from 'A Remembered Harvest'

I had watched from the early time of the year the cultivation of the hops, involving a variety of skills, from the ploughing with horses between the 'hills' – the perennial hop plants of which nothing could be seen in winter but the slightly rounded mounds stretching away in symmetrical rows – to the delicate 'twiddling' of the bines when the shoots appeared and had to be trained to the strings which had already been stretched criss-cross from pole to pole. The strings made an intricate design, seeming to envelop the garden in a glowing mist.

But it is the great festival of the year on our farm that I want to recall, for it had a pagan quality, age-old and primitive, which especially appealed to me. The strings, by this time late in August, were covered with the harsh hop bines and their golden pungent fruit hanging in bountiful garlands among the dark leaves. This was the time for the harvesting of the hops – more like flowers than fruit, with petals overlapping. Under the green arches, canvas troughs slung on rough wooden frames were placed in rows some feet apart, but close enough for the pickers to chat and exchange jokes and gossip with each other.

The picking on our farm was done by village women and children; the garden was not large enough for the need of 'east-enders', who emigrated in their thousands to other parts of Kent from Lambeth and Whitechapel to spend six weeks in the Kent clay to replenish their marvellous vitality. For us the only men to give zest to the bawdy jokes which the atmosphere of this work evoked, even in the most chapel-minded women, were the tally-men, perhaps six to this small garden. These men had much to do. It was their job to cut, with the razor-edged sickle-shaped knife at the end of a long pole, the bines from the strings and drape these armfuls of hop-laden tendrils over the bar of wood raised above the trough so that the pickers could loosen the tangle and rob its fruit, dropping each hop separately – never in bunches – into the bin.

I was there with my maid, Daisy Turner, and my two children: Bronwen only a baby and carried by one of us, and Merfyn, a sturdy boy of four. When the ceremony began (hop-picking had its strict etiquette and procedure) each trough had already been garlanded by its share of bines and beside each waited the women and their families. Until the tally-man blew his horn not a hop might be picked, and in those faraway days law and order entered into every department of life. Especially, I think, was this so in those activities closely related to the earth. Even in the wild prodigality of nature there is a rhythm and order

Country People

with which the countryman is instinct. So that the heady smell of hops and the freedom from the indoor chores evoked in the women an element of licentiousness and all went as merrily as a marriage bell during those golden revels.

The horn having sounded we fell to our picking and this was done by experienced women, who from babyhood had been trained in this skill, with delicate neatness and swiftness. The hops that fell into the bin had to be clean of any leaf and of each other. It took me a long time to learn how to do this. The hop fruit is a cone of petals, and the skilled picker will manage to detach one from its bunch whole and compact without, as I often did, scattering the fruit in a flurry of petals into the bin. Children sat on little stools or piles of coats with a box or bucket or perhaps a hat between their chubby knees. Their mothers would throw them bunches of hops to pick and when their buckets were full they would proudly add the contents to the mounting mass in the bin.

The tally-man would come round and cry, 'Pick up yer 'ops!' Especially with inexperienced pickers and children some hops were dropped on the ground, and each had to be retrieved, for there must be no waste and no untidiness in this harvest. With him the women would bandy words, and always there was a hilarious and pretended enmity between them and this master of ceremonials, and though Daisy would laugh uproariously at some of the bawdiness, it was so new to me I did not understand it at all, but I knew by the quality of the laughter and the look in the eyes of the jokers that the ribaldry was of the dark earth of which I, town-bred and innocent, knew nothing.

At noon the horn would sound and we must finish picking the bine we had in hand, for to begin a new one was forbidden. Now the tally-man came with his bushel-basket to measure the hops each picker had in her trough, and with a lovely gesture the women plunged their arms deep into their cargo and with a sort of flutter of the hands and fingers raised the heavy load to let the air and space into their packing, so that the precious fruit would go lightly into the tally-man's measure and pile up to the bushel mark more quickly. With what keen eyes they watched his measure, for pay was by the bushel. I think the pay for my pick entered in the tally-man's book was sixpence.

Now with our appetites whetted by the heady hop-impregnated air we sat around our bins for lunch. This consisted of the traditional bottles of cold tea and slabs of baked bread-pudding full of fruit and brown sugar, sticky and extremely satisfying. We sat on the hard clay, enjoying the food and laughing and talking. The children got restive when they had eaten their fill and played hide-and-seek in the still untouched bowers, and the suckled babies were changed and put back in their prams. The women's rough and golden-stained hands were for a moment idle. Looking away down the avenue of green leaves I could glimpse brightly coloured groups of women and children in attitudes of repose and presently a silence would fall under that fruit-laden darkness of leaves and the children would curl up by their mothers and sleep, and the women unused to idleness, would nod. The tally-men lay flat out on their backs with heads resting on their upraised hands, and there would be no sound but the murmur of insects and distant lowing of cattle.

Such a scene, such a quality of living enriched my spirit for ever.

Helen Thomas
(1977 - 1967)

UNDER STORM'S WING

There is an air of fulfilment and rest in the landscape and brooding weather of October. It is like a ghost of summer evening all the time; the faint spears of shadow, the sun's shield tarnished and hanging low, and under the trees, instead of shade, pools of their fallen colours. The fields, being mostly stubble, have still the straw-gold light of summer, but the ploughs move there, as in the very afterglow of harvest, and the earth is gradually revealed again that has not been seen since spring. Other men are at work cementing and closing in the gains of the year against the weather turning enemy. The thatcher mounts his ladder many times with his burden of straw, roofing the corn built to be its own storehouse: over the hedge, the spade of the man earthing up the root-clamp is visible at moments; with regular rhythm it appears suddenly, slaps a slab of grey clay upon the straw, and vanishes for another, till the long hump is a fort against frost, neatly moated, too, where the earth has been cut out. The hedger is there also, defeating the hedge in its summer attempt to usurp a yard of the field all around; it is still warm enough for shirt-sleeves, working, and he is a summer figure yet. The farmer, with his gun and dog, is walking the stubble for partridges before they get too wild, to prove to himself that he has not lost his aim since January last, nor his dog her nose. As to the city man his tennis-racquet as he takes it down on a summer's evening, his business done, so to the farmer his gun in the evening glow of autumn. He goes out with it, but for survey of his fields as much as to shoot. He never closes both eyes to his job. The eye he doesn't aim with is seeing that another harrowing is necessary here for wheat.

Adrian Bell
(1901 – 1980)

Silver Ley

October

Nature now spreads around, in dreary hue
A pall to cover all that summer knew;
Yet, in the poet's solitary way,
Some pleasing objects for his praise delay,
Something that will make him pause and turn again,
As every trifle will his eye detain: ...
The hedger stopping gaps, amid the leaves,
Which time, o'erhead, in every colour weaves;
The milkmaid stepping with a timid look,
From stone to stone, across the brimming brook,
The cotter journeying with his noisy swine,
Along the woodside where the brambles twine,
Shaking from mossy oaks the acorns brown,
Or from the hedges red haws dashing down;
The nutters rustling in the yellow woods,
Who tease the wild things in their solitude;
The hunters, from their thicket's avenue,
In scarlet jackets, startling on the view,
Skimming a moment o'er the russet plain,
Then hiding in the motley woods again;
The plopping sun's sharp momentary shock,
Which Echo bustles from her cave to mock; ...
The village dames, as they get ripe and fine,
Gather the bunches for their "eldern wine",
Which, bottled up, becomes a rousing charm,
To kindle winter's icy bosom warm
And, with its merry partner, nut-brown beer,
Makes up the peasant's Christmas-keeping cheer.

John Clare
(1793 – 1864)

from A *Shepherd's Calendar*

Country People

HOME AND GARDEN

Sabine's duties were by no means confined to the purely ornamental. Country households in the sixteenth century were almost completely self-supporting as far as the necessaries of life were concerned, relying on their own resources for food and drink, clothes and fuel. Sabine had to look after all the household, doctor their ailments as well as she could with herbal remedies, and sometimes scold them into common sense. She had to supervise the work of the house, the inevitable dusting and polishing and cleaning, the washing and ironing, the sewing and spinning; she had to arrange the menu for the week's meals, the breakfasts and dinners and suppers that the entire household sat down to, and all the baking and brewing that went on; there was the cultivation of the flower and vegetable gardens to attend to, and the dairy as well, the milking and cheese-making, the butter-churning and cream-skimming, the feeding of the pigs and poultry, the egg collecting, and the marketing of all the surplus produce at Oundle market. Besides this she ran the big farm in John's absence from home, directing the wool-buying and winding and sheep-shearing, buying cattle and horses, collecting the tithes and rents, seeing to the repairs of the barns and houses, paying the bills and keeping the accounts, and looking after village affairs generally. If Sabine was occasionally out of temper, it is hardly to be wondered at.

Barbara Winchester
(b.1924)

TUDOR FAMILY PORTRAIT

When, a few years afterwards, he inherited Saltram, and he and Theresa were married, John Parker was already, therefore, a man of mature experience, of substantial property and responsibility, and established in politics. He was thirty-five. Theresa was ten years younger – but, despite her relative youthfulness, a woman of mature judgement. Together, with a shared enjoyment and enthusiasm, they gave their minds to the reshaping of Saltram; to continuing the improvements to the house which Lady Catherine had so substantially begun.

Their own interest lay chiefly in certain internal alterations: the making of a great Drawing Room, on which they were to spend something like £10,000; the improvement of the Library – which was later changed into an Eating Room; and on internal decorations, and the building up of a good collection of paintings. Even so, there was also a good deal of outside building. The stable block was completed. The 'Castle', a pleasant summer retreat designed (in its interior) by Robert Adam; the delightful Orangery; the greenhouse; and a new Stag entrance and Lodges; were all planned and begun. It was a busy and enjoyable time. Only two years after their marriage, Theresa wrote to Fritz:

The Hot Houses, Kitchen Gardens are just finished. The Castle, the other lodges and a Green House employ the next year, and after that we turn farmer and make such improvements in Land, Estates, and Ploughs that Posterity shall bless the day… (And, one year later:) All our building draws very near a conclusion … though a new Eating Room is thought of at a distance.

Ronald Fletcher
(1921 – 1992)

THE PARKERS AT SALTRAM

As the last dead leaves of winter are scoured from tree and hedge by the March winds; as the last seed pods rattle their emptiness on the bean trellis; as the gutters and ditches are cleansed of winter's dross by spring rains, man too feels the need to share in the cleansing process. The home, too much lived in through the winter days, has become prison-like. There is a need to open windows now and let in air and light; and to add colour in the home to vie with the burgeoning spring outside. The village resounds with dull thwacks as carpets are lifted, hung on clothes lines and beaten till all the dust (and some say the devil too) is beaten out of them. Up and down the village, washday now assumes monstrous proportions, as curtains, underblankets and mattress covers join the regular items. Nor is the need for 'a good blow' confined to Mondays. The really zealous women take weeks over their purge, giving as much care to reading the weather as the Romans did to examining entrails, as a guide to major enterprises. Patched and very worn articles are dried at night. Fine things are hung out by day, and left on view long after they are dry. The local shops run short of borax and soap, and even the rough women are civil to the local carrier, on whom they rely to fetch their goods from town.

Mrs. Swingler, our washerwoman, normally comes only on a Monday. Now Mother hires her for a week. The menfolk in our house know that during that time life will be unbearable.

The women are important as at no other time in the year and they know it! Virtue is on their side, and any inconvenience they inflict is twice blessed: it is necessary, and it lets the men know that running a house doesn't just mean 'flicking a feather duster'. Just occasionally we are hailed from the farmyard to move heavy furniture, but large and by we try to escape to the comparative predictability of pigs, cows and sheep. We are ordered (not asked) to keep cattle out of the orchard in case they bring the clothes lines down, and if we see storm clouds to announce the fact immediately.

Mrs. Swingler's arms go redder as the days go by and her arm muscles bulge through much twisting of dolly pegs and turning of the mangle. Occasionally she appears in the orchard with a clothes basket on her hip, as washing appears and disappears. Even our man, who usually swears at Mrs Swingler because she's deaf, has a good word to say for her. In the house, ceilings are white-washed and walls colour-washed or re-papered. Bedroom floors are scrubbed, windows re-painted inside, and mouse-holes stopped up. The brass knobs on the bed ends shine like burnished gold. Wardrobes are turned out and re-papered inside with wallpaper remnants. We retire to bed in an aura of mothballs, carbolic soap and disinfectant.

Downstairs the purge is even more thorough. New coco-matting appears in the kitchen, the couch is re-covered in velvet, and Father's armchair has a new cushion and back-drape. New backing paper is placed behind the bacon flitches in the kitchen to prevent grease messing up the wallpaper. The carpenter planes the top of the kitchen table where twelve months of scrubbing has left hard grain and knots protruding. The oak beams in all rooms are re-stained a rich brown. Even the dog kennel is re-covered with felt and creosoted to kill the fleas.

By the end of March the deed is done. Visitors entering the house wrinkle an appreciative nose and say, 'My word you do smell clean.'

Harold Cramp
(b.1912)

Yeoman's Farmer's Son

It is an unruly Cornish garden, sloped, with granite rocks and steep paths dark with yews, its beds tangled with flowers. Cornish gardens are famous for their flowers – half Mrs. Quin's neighbours in the big houses live by selling theirs, specialising in parma violets, arum lilies, mimosa, rhododendrons, 'but not your mother,' says Walter to Bella sarcastically, 'nothing half as useful.'

'A garden isn't meant to be useful. It's a joy,' says Mrs Quin. To watch her among her flowers is, as John Henry her husband says, like watching a scholar in his library who, as he talks, goes to one shelf or another, pulling out a book to show, to brood over or to read from. Mrs Quin, each time she comes in from the garden, has a leaf, a flower or a bud in her hand: a berry with a spider's web, seeds that she will put in saucers on the window-sills, a spray of bergamot to smell or a new African day lily of which someone has sent her a root that autumn; sometimes it is an especially well-formed rose, or a tendril of briony. 'You are like the householder in the Bible,' says Cecily.

'The householder?' asks Mrs Quin, puzzled, but Cecily, being Chapel, is well versed in texts and cannot be shaken. 'The householder which bringeth forth out of his treasure things old and new.'

Rumer Godden
(1907 – 1998)

CHINA COURT

CORN AND HAY

All afternoon and evening we worked in the cornfield, stooking the crop which was to feed our little stock, and so, indirectly, man during the coming year. The machines for cutting and binding had arrived late, and several days of a week of sunshine had been lost waiting for them; the air was translucent and the distant horizon of cliffs and sea so beautiful that the thought of rain was never far away. We therefore worked urgently, following close in the sweeping tracks of the binder, moving slowly in from the wide circumference towards the narrowing heart of shimmering corn. None of us, save the men on the machines, were very experienced in the art, but, knowing what depended on it, we worked with a will and with that steady unceasing compulsion which all work with a living nature seems to necessitate. The goal in our minds was not the hour at which labour ceased, but the completion of the work, the last stook stacked, the fields clear and garnered. Even the beauty of the scene was incidental. Only occasionally did we raise our eyes from that high, slanting field, sparkling and rustling in sun and wind, to take in the wonderful panorama below: the old grey house, with its William and Mary red brick chimneys rising out of the trees, the green clay pastures stretching to the margin of the sea, and the tawny downs, the jagged cliffs of shale, limestone and chalk spread in fantastic panorama from Broad Bench to Ringstead, the blue of Weymouth Bay and Portland lying like a distant giant floating on the bosom of the Channel, the high, white clouds driving like solitary galleons out of the west. No more beautiful setting to the husbandman's business can have ever existed, and, as the shadows lengthened and the rooks began to wheel home, its loveliness and peace surpassed the human power of description. Our throats and lips were parched, our feet battered by the iron, uneven ground, our bodies pierced with innumerable spear-points of oats and barley, but, as the corn vanished and the stooks rose, in sunlight, twilight and, last of all, in moonlight, a feeling of aching triumph and satisfaction overcame weariness. We had been all-day participants in a battle and it was nearly over. The enemy, next winter's want, on our little piece of the farming front – all that we could see and experience – was in retreat. A victory had been won.

Arthur Bryant
(1899 - 1985)

THE LION AND THE UNICORN

In haytime we were more busy than in corn harvest, for the farm having a lot of grass-land, we mowed a fair lot of hay, besides having a field of clover. I used to turn out quite early in the morning when cutting grass, as the machine cuts better while the dew is on, besides being easier for the horses before the sun gets powerful. Several mornings I reached the field as the church clock was striking five, and I know of no pleasanter occupation than to be mowing grass at that hour, when the sun is scarcely touching the dew-drops, and not a soul about; with a stray partridge calling up its chicks, and a blackie piping atop of the ash-tree. Maybe a magpie will come scolding, for he thinks it an offence for these humans to come disturbing him before it is well daylight. Then, it seems, you see the earth as God made it.

There is something fascinating, almost evil, about the grass reaper; unlike the binder that waits for the corn to die and then reaps, it cuts through life, sweeping down the slender moon-pennies and toppling them over into long lines of swathes, desecrating beds of royal purple. It chatters its way through tangles of wild vetches, and leaves behind it long lines of trembling grass, cocksfoot, and white clover. By seven o'clock the sun gets higher and all the grasses shimmer in drops of crystal, and the skylark dries his dewy wings in the sun, and in the shady wood the pigeons croon a drowsy note, and all the air is full of scents and hazy mists and humming bees. Another scorching day is here. Then you look at your work, and say, 'It is enough,' and go home to breakfast.

So I reaped in the early morning, and after breakfast hoed turnips, or turned the hay I had reaped the day before; and when the hay was ready, built it into neat stacks, working until nine at night, and finding days all too short because life was good.

Fred Kitchen
(b.1891)

BROTHER TO THE OX

When at last the great day dawns, the Commander musters his crew, an ex-Marine and a retired naval rating, who, like himself, are nearer seventy than sixty years of age. With shirt sleeves rolled up, and his cap at a Beatty angle, the Commander runs a thumb across the gleaming scythe. Equidistant to port and starboard, the two hands wait a yard astern of their master. 'Right!' One word suffices. The pageant begins.

There are many books about mowing, but only music can evoke the slow-motion sculpture of mowers and the rhythmic sibilance of scythes. Mowing is a type of rustic ballet, comparable with poplars swaying on a breeze. The act itself is so easy that centuries of simple men have mastered it, yet so difficult that an urban learner has been known to topple over at the first stroke and to gash his ankle at the second.

J.H.B. Peel
(1913 – 1983)

New Country Talk

Hulton Getty Picture Collection

Country People

FRUIT AND VEGETABLES

Mr Rudge continues to live – or at least to exist – on his plums. It is, he admits, a somewhat chancy business. When there are plenty of them they sell for as little as one-and sixpence a pot of seventy-two pounds: when they sell for twenty-four shillings a pot they are usually so scarce that it makes little difference. If you grow early varieties, they have to compete with imports from France and Italy. If you grow late ones, they come in at a time when everybody has eaten so many plums that they are sick of the sight of them. If there is a glut, the canners and bottlers are in a position to beat you down. If they are scarce they are in a position to do exactly the same, having canned or bottled all they need in the last year of plenty. These are not idle statements. Mr Rudge can prove them by figures, and is always ready to do so on the least provocation.

He is still, in spite of his numerous ambitious failures which include, in addition to these, disastrous adventures in jam-making, rhubarb-forcing and mushroom-growing – an incurable optimist. He no longer has the air of adventurous prosperity he wore when he first came to Monk's Norton. His clothes are threadbare; his neck has the skinny look of a plucked chicken; his whole body looks somehow shrunken except his little pot belly, which is spanned by a silver watch-chain. He is rather hard of hearing – even the Captain has to shout when he 'pops in' for a smoke of an evening – and his eyes are not quite what they were. Yet, from first to last, his hope and enthusiasm have never wavered. Though he has given up trying to make a fortune for himself on the land he can still demonstrate mathematically exactly how it can be done. And whether you make a fortune or not, he will tell you, no life can compare with that of the small-holder.

Francis Brett Young
(1884 - 1954)

PORTRAIT OF A VILLAGE

I was very fortunate in coming on the strawberry farmer just as the fruit was ripening. He was a recent settler, a sympathetic simple-life soul, a sick-of-the-town, ashamed-of-the-war young man. He was alone on his farm, and welcomed me to a pitch on one of his grassy paths, and also to help gather in the harvest. I stayed for several days, and learned what a welter of excitement there is behind that cool and refreshing fruit. It is a wild and hazardous business, this strawberry farming. All the year coaxing and cultivating the little plants, waiting and hoping (and hoeing) for a couple of weeks of fine weather to prevail at just the right time for ripening and gathering the fruit. And if the weather fail – well, then the crop fails, and one must wait and hoe, with empty pockets, for better fortune next year.

My host had two fields of plants, but in one only were the berries ripening early and fetching a good price. The other field was a nightmare. There were plenty of berries on the plants, but development was held up for want of rain. One good shower and the fruit would plump up, ripen, and be a success, but if the dry weather continued it would never mature, and I cannot say how many pounds' worth of fruit would be lost to the market. A life of high hopes and sudden fortune, or – failure. There was an air of tragedy when I arrived in this six-acre world of strawberries. There was a feeling of do or die, and I was carried into the business on the urgent current.

With the next day just dawning, and half a sun blazing over the hedge at the bottom of the field, we commenced picking. There was a wonderful silence and a dewy freshness in the morning air. Only the sun seemed alive, a large, ardent sun rising with enormous purpose. A cock crowed, a bird or two twittered, and away on the road was the sound of a trotting horse. We had a bundle of strawberry baskets, 'chips' they call them, on our backs, and with one in our hands we stooped over the low plants to gather the luscious harvest. The bottom of the basket was soon covered; we picked briskly and the gathering mounted up. I was tempted by a large berry, very red and dropping with ripeness. At that hour of the morning, fresh from the plant, the strawberry is a miracle, it is all fragrance and sweetness – an ineffable nectar – a present from the gods, and you realize that there can be such a thing as perfection in this wicked world.

The first basket was soon filled with its load of three pounds and left standing on the straw between the lines of plants. A new chip must be unslung from the back, and another three pounds begins to mount up. By this time I was beginning to consider which was the easiest and most comfortable way of picking – so soon does the human creature begin to plot and scheme after its comforts. I stooped and squatted, and knelt first on one knee, then the other, and then both; I walked from plant to plant, wriggled and shuffled along on the knees. By the time the second basket was full I realized that all the positions were equally uncomfortable.

But we stuck to our picking. Prices were good that morning, and at eight o'clock the collecting van would call. We worked systematically up and down the long lines of the field, leaving, here and there, the full baskets standing in the straw. It was hard work, but engrossing and attractive. More and more the strawberry plant impresses you with its wonder – its stalks curving out gracefully from the centre and the decorative leaves poised over the berries with a conscious, almost a maternal air. The plants yield their fruit easily and seem to rustle their leaves into order again as you pass. And I wondered, kneeling close to the plants, if they could feel anything of the pride and satisfaction of creation, or be at all conscious of joy or pain at parting with their offspring. Plant after plant, each had its character, and I was amused to find myself feeling on quite intimate terms with certain of them, for I could see that each of them had enjoyed their different adventures.

And in between the strawberry plants were weeds with bright flowers – the scarlet pimpernel, the blue speedwell, all sorts of little coloured stars and bells, with a reflective grasshopper clinging in some ridiculous position; and then 'twas a spider, an ant, or a glistening beetle. Stooping over them continuously one wandered in a faerie world of small flowers and dewdrops, of fruits and fantastic creatures – a sunny world, that morning, all brightness and fragrance.

Walter Wilkinson
(1875 - 1943)

VAGABONDS AND PUPPETS

In an excellent growing season with just the right amount of bright sun, warm nights and gentle rain when it was required, vegetables throughout the North West grew splendidly that year. Bolstered up by the dung, even our thin land provided reasonably heavy crops because the weather was so much in their favour. But, under such circumstances, every pound of extra yield and every fraction of a penny gained by being a day or two earlier in the market is vital if vegetable growing is to pay.

My yields were heavy enough to make me nearly scream with pain as the result of bending to collect them until the last glimmer of daylight had gone. However, they were no heavier or earlier than those obtained by more experienced men on better land. By July the work trap into which I had fallen became pitifully obvious. Large, tight-headed, flawless white cauliflowers were selling for less than half a new penny each. Lush green, crumbly edged savoys which occupied a whole square yard of ground, pretty as a cabbage rose, did no better a month later.

Fine sprouts in November, or broccoli in the following March, sold equally poorly and did nothing to compensate for the ludicrous twelve new pence per hundred-weight sack which was the best we could obtain for our usual low crop of potatoes.

Tom Williamson could only commiserate when we realised that my plan had failed. I mustn't be too discouraged, he insisted, pointing out that even at those prices, the land had made a better contribution to our income than it might have done in other crops. I knew that what he said was true. The country was still in the depths of the depression. Eggs had tumbled from seven and half to four pence a dozen. Cheese was down to a derisory three and a half new pence a pound and all other farm prices reflected the same situation.

I was so depressed that it was perhaps only Tom's own courageous example which helped me to face another even more disastrous farming year.

Arthur Hollins
(b.1915)

THE FARMER, THE PLOUGH AND THE DEVIL

Under the wall was a large patch recently dug, beside the patch a grass path, and on the path a wheelbarrow. A man was busy putting in potatoes; he wore the raggedest coat ever seen on a respectable back. As the wind lifted the tails it was apparent that the lining was loose and only hung by threads, the ruffs were worn through, there was a hole beneath each arm, and on each shoulder the nap of the cloth was gone; the colour, which had once been grey, was now a mixture of several soils and numerous kinds of grit. The hat he had on was no better; it might have been made of some hard pasteboard, it was so bare. Every now and then the wind brought a few handfuls of dust over the wall from the road, and dropped it on his stooping back.

The way in which he was planting potatoes was wonderful, every potato was placed at exactly the right distance apart, and a hole made for it in a general trench; before it was set it was looked at and turned over, and the thumb rubbed against it to be sure that it was sound, and when finally put in, a little mound was delicately adjusted round to keep it in its right position till the whole row was buried. He carried the potatoes in his coat pocket – those, that is, for the row – and took them out one by one; had he been planting his own children he could not have been more careful. The science, the skill, and the experience brought, to this potato-planting you would hardly credit; for all this care was founded upon observation, and arose from very large abilities on the part of the planter, though directed to so humble a purpose at that moment.

Richard Jefferies
(1848 – 1887)

AMARYLLIS AT THE FAIR

MILK AND BUTTER

The dairy maids and men had flocked down from their cottages and out of the dairy-house with the arrival of the cows from the meads; the maids walking in pattens, not on account of the weather, but to keep their shoes above the mulch of the barton. Each girl sat down on her three-legged stool, her face sideways, her right cheek resting against the cow, and looked musingly along the animal's flank at Tess as she approached. The male milkers, with hat-brims turned down, resting flat on their foreheads and gazing on the ground, did not observe her.

One of these was a sturdy middle-aged man – whose long white 'pinner' was somewhat finer and cleaner than the wraps of the others, and whose jacket underneath had a presentable

marketing aspect – the master-dairyman, of whom she was in quest, his double character as a working milker and butter-maker here during six days, and on the seventh as a man in shining broad cloth in his family pew at church, being so marked as to have inspired a rhyme –

> Dairyman Dick
> All the week:
> On Sundays Mister Richard Crick.

Seeing Tess standing at gaze he went across to her.

'Well, I suppose you'll want a dish o' tay, or victuals of some sort, hey? Not yet? Well, do as ye like about it. But faith, if 'twas I, I should be as dry as a kex wi' travelling so far.'

'I'll begin milking now, to get my hand in,' said Tess …

She drank a little milk as temporary refreshment − to the surprise − indeed, slight contempt − of Dairyman Crick, to whose mind it had apparently never occurred that milk was good as a beverage.

'Oh, if ye can swaller that, be it so,' he said indifferently, while holding up the pail that she sipped from. ''Tis what I hadn't touched for years − not I. Rot the stuff; it would lie in my innerds like lead. You can try your hand upon she,' he pursued, nodding to the nearest cow. 'Not but what she do milk rather hard. We've hard ones and we've easy ones, like other folks. However, you'll find out that soon enough.'

When Tess had changed her bonnet for a hood, and was really on her stool under the cow, and the milk was squirting from her fists into the pail, she appeared to feel that she really had laid a new foundation for her future. The conviction bred serenity, her pulse slowed, and she was able to look about her.

The milkers formed quite a little battalion of men and maids, the men operating on the hard-teated animals, the maids on the kindlier natures. It was a large dairy. There were nearly a hundred milkers under Crick's management, all told; and of the herd the master-dairyman milked six or eight with his own hands, unless away from home.

Thomas Hardy
(1840 − 1923)

TESS OF THE D'URBERVILLES

Hetty's was a springtide beauty; it was the beauty of young frisking things, round-limbed, gambolling, circumventing you by a false air of innocence – the innocence of a young star-browed calf, for example, that, being inclined for a promenade out of bounds, leads you a severe steeplechase over hedge and ditch, and only comes to a stand in the middle of a bog.

And they are the prettiest attitudes and movements into which a pretty girl is thrown in making up butter – tossing movements that give a charming curve to the arm, and a sideward inclination of the round white neck; little patting and rolling movements with the palm of the hand, and nice adaptations and finishings which cannot at all be effected without a great play of the pouting mouth and the dark eyes. And then the butter itself seems to communicate a fresh charm – it is so pure, so sweet-scented; it is turned off the mould with such a beautiful, firm surface, like marble in a pale yellow light! Moreover, Hetty was particularly clever at making up the butter; it was the one performance of hers that her aunt allowed to pass without severe criticism, so she handled it with all the grace that belongs to mastery.

George Eliot
(1819 – 1880)

Adam Bede

CHAIRS AND CROOKS

I was taken to call at a thatched cottage beyond the village green, and received a warm welcome from the chair-maker and his wife. He was a little old man of eighty-one with a bright eye and an impish face. I thought of the bored young men one encounters around club bars, who wonder at thirty how they will continue to get through the next twelve months. The old man was so alert, and had so many facts of interest to impart, that I had to pin him down question by question.

He shocked me a little by the delight with which he produced a newly turned leg of a chair. His grandson had taken him to a furniture factory in High Wycombe, and had shown him a German lathe. Would I believe it, asked the old man excitedly, fifty chair legs had been turned out in one minute, and they had lathes to make a thousand an hour! He pointed out, with a pride that sprang from his own craftsmanship, that the lathe making such a leg must have had at least seven chisels. 'Why, it would 'ave tekken me half an' hour to do it. That machine's better than thirty of us!'

There was one feature in which this kind of turning was better than machine turning. To-day, the wood must go to the factory; before, the lathe went to the wood. It was the habit of the chair-maker to buy a 'fall' of beech, and set up his lathe at the side of the trunk, sawing off and splitting piece by piece as he needed it. The old chair-maker showed me a photograph of half a dozen turners sitting by their machines in the heart of the wood.

I asked him if there were any chair-makers working the pole lathe now.

'Only a few. Them machines in Wycombe's killed 'em all. They won't know what a pole-lathe is in ten years. I reckon that lathe o' mine ought to go in a museum, an' me with it!'

He gave a chuckle at this. His grandson, smartly dressed for the town, wheeled a motor-cycle out of the yard and started it up with a roar.

'That's what everybody wants nowadays – they won't want chairs at all soon, they'll have forgotten how to sit!'

Cecil Roberts
(1892 – 1976)

GONE RUSTIC

I went to see Mitchell of Pyecombe, the last of the Sussex crook-makers, in his sixteenth century barn-smithy. His father had been a blacksmith — he died at ninety-eight — and his grandfather a wheelwright, so that his craftsmanship was bred in the bone. He told me that there were now only forty-five apprentices for the smiths of the whole United Kingdom. 'You don't mean to tell me you still make crooks?' 'A few.' 'But the sheep have left the downs.' 'Oh, I don't make 'em for shepherds, only for bishops.' With a resigned irony he quoted me what he had read in Gilbert White, that 'no self-respecting Sussex shepherd should be without a Pycombe crook.' He had had one order from the Bishop of Tristan da Cunha, but, since these crooks have become an ecclesiastical monopoly, he could not make one for the great sheepless shoulder of down opposite his smithy. He remembered a thousand Southdowns grazing on it. He remembered the days when farmers farmed, not just pulled teats and emptied the chemical bag. A man, he said, could in the old days walk for nine miles on the Downs from Pyecombe to Lewes on a sward 'like a billiard table.' Now the grass is up to the knees.

H.J. Massingham
(1888 - 1952)

WHERE MAN BELONGS

I paid Tom off, who then betook himself to the outhouse of his cottage till another job turned up, or work in the woods began again, whittling away at walking-sticks there in the meantime. Always as he worked in the woods he had an eye for a likely bit of ash or thorn, and the rafters of his shed were hung with hundreds of them seasoning and awaiting his days of idleness. Then he would polish their bark, and for some make knobs decorated with poker-work designs, while the ends of others he would hold over scalding steam and bend into crooks. Sometimes Nature herself would offer a freakish suggestion. Here, say, was a thorn that grew complete with a queer knobby handle. By deft carving he would accentuate the knobbiness into a comic, snoutish face.

He walked great distances, taking a bundle of sticks into a wayside inn when the men were gathered for the evening, laying three on the table. Each man would stake twopence, and the matter would be decided on the quoit board, the winner taking his choice of the sticks, and the next two in their order. Tom would pocket the stakes, take up his sticks and stir his stumps to the next inn along the road.

The farmers would often hail him with, 'Got a new stick for me, Tom?' Many a hall-stand in the vicinity was a museum-case of his quaint craftsmanship.

I have one which I prize, I have grown so familiar with it. It has been so many miles with me; a rough thing, all notches. Tom did not think it a good effort of his – 'Very homely' – but to me it has a satisfying look. When we were working at the laid corn Nora used to bring us tea at five o'clock, and on the last day of harvest Tom produced a stick which he presented to her. Now, his homely sticks were, as I say, admirable, but Nora being a 'lady,' and the occasion being a special one, he had been to great pains to make the gift, as he thought, suitable. He had chosen a slender stick, smoothed it, and coated it with sticky-looking red varnish – more, he had cut a strip of tin, and nailed it round in imitation of the silver band that decorates the shopman's article. The effect was deplorable, but of course Nora had to be extravagant in her admiration and thanks, for obviously he thought it the finest stick he had ever made.

Adrian Bell
(1901 – 1980)

THE CHERRY TREE

HARNESS AND HORSESHOES

Another character in my life was the saddler who lived near the rectory, William ('Codger') Saddington. His shop, a few yards beyond, was full of interest for me and full of rubbish besides. I spent hours just watching him work. He was a master craftsman with leather. He did practically all the harness and saddlery in the village. The shop was a fine example of orderly chaos, yet old Codger could put his hand on any particular piece he required at once. He was a master at plaiting and spent quite a time trying to teach me. He had examples of any number of plaits. The tools of his trade always fascinated me. He had a large mallet made from lignum vitae, a very hard wood which he used for beating the leather and which had a very high polish. I used to hang on to this all the time I was in the shop. We could buy hanks of whipcord for a penny. We were regularly replacing the whipcord on the hunting crops, as much for the sake of doing it rather than because it was required. There was a certain way of doing it. Father, Tim and George were good at it but if mine did not please me I would take it down to Codger who would oblige. He made up his sewing threads by twisting several strands of thin string or thick cotton and waxing with cobbler's wax. This gave a very strong material and anything Codger sewed rarely came apart.

Aubrey Moore
(1893 - 1992)

SON OF A RECTORY

Timmy is the last harness maker in Cappaghlas. When he goes there won't be any to follow because no one is doing the apprenticeship any more. His small shop backs off the main street, and in spite of the changed times, there always seems to be a pile of old harness bundled in the corner waiting to be repaired. Most of his business is mending – shoes, bridles, anything leather.

He is a small grey-haired man who wears glasses and looks down at you like an absent-minded professor. All the time his hands are busy sewing at the leather. He isn't altogether sad at the harness maker's demise – stitching eight hours a day wore your arms down. A lot of people talk about old crafts, but you can be sure of one thing, Timmy will say, that they never put an hour's work into them. If they had, most likely they would be talking differently.

Peter Somerville-Large
(b.1928)

CAPPAGHLAS

The Village Blacksmith

Under a spreading chestnut-tree
The village smithy stands;
The smith, a mighty man is he
With large and sinewy hands;
And the muscles of his brawny arms
Are strong as iron bands...

Week in, week out, from morn till night,
You can hear his bellows blow;
You can hear him swing his heavy sledge,
With measured beat and slow,
Like a sexton ringing the village bell,
When the evening sun is low.

And children coming home from school
Look in at the open door;
They love to see the flaming forge,
And hear the bellows roar,
And catch the burning sparks that fly
Like chaff from a threshing floor.

Henry Wadsworth Longfellow
(1807 – 1882)

WHEELS AND WAGONS

His drinking bouts were not very frequent, or perhaps he would not have been the good craftsman he was. For William Hart, during the first twenty years of his working life, practised the trade of a wheelwright, and he made better wagons than anybody else between Birmingham and Bristol. You can see

them still if you visit the neighbourhood of Brensham – for they were made to last for ever – and at farm sales the auctioneer still draws attention to them, urging the company to bid an extra five pounds. 'Come, come, gentlemen, this is no ordinary job. None of your gimcrack jerrybuilt contraptions here. This is a William Hart wagon – see the name on it! These wheels will still be going round when you're in the churchyard.' They were mostly big wagons designed for carrying hay; Mr Hart always spoke of them as wains and himself as a wainwright. Nowadays most farmers use a haysweep instead to bring the hay to the rick (or they bale it on the ground, so that they do not need to rick it at all) and the wagons stand disused and neglected in rickyards and homesteads, but they never fall to pieces, and the bright yellow paint on them (three coats of it) doesn't flake off like modern paint – you can spot them from a mile away.

It used to take William Hart the better part of a month to make a wagon. He built each with loving care, choosing and seasoning the timber himself, and taking infinite pains over every joint, hinge and spoke. ('Measure twice and cut once,' he always used to say.) But as soon as it was done, the moment he'd crossed the 't' of the 'W. Hart' which although he could only read and write with difficulty he stencilled so neatly on the side of it – as soon as he'd done that he went down to the pub and got drunk. He would come bursting into the bar, and order drinks all round, with that transcendent air of blessed relaxation and utter abandon which artists know when they have put the finishing touches to a work of creation and, all passion spent, allow the tide of life to bear them where it will. Usually he stayed drunk for about a week, and it was another ten days before he regained complete sobriety. So, with repairs and odd-jobs and a bit of undertaking – it was said that his pride of craftsmanship made him take as much trouble over a coffin for his worst enemy as over a wagon for his best friend – he built about eight of his great haywains in a year. This earned him ample money for his needs.

John Moore
(1907 - 1967)

THE BLUE FIELD

One of the unforgettable characters of my childhood was Mr. Busby. His bill-heads boasted, and with good reason, that he was 'Frank Zacharias Busby, Wheelwright, Joiner, Painter, Decorator and Undertaker'. Locals called him Zach. Befitting a man with such Biblical overtones, he was a pillar of the church. It also seemed appropriate that my father and he should always address one another as 'neighbour', a form of address used nowhere else in the village. Zach's house and workshops lay at the bottom of the village about a hundred yards from our farmhouse. But to visit them was to enter another world. Entrance to his property put me in mind of entering a castle. His house was linked to a neighbouring one by an arch over which was a bedroom. The arch was big enough to admit the largest farm wagons and led to a spacious yard. One side was flanked by a wing of the house and extending from it was a long range of buildings.

First came the wheelwright's shed round which was ranged every item that goes to make a wheel: seasoned wood, spokes, fellies, hubs, hub caps and iron rims. There was usually a wheel on the floor, assembled in all particulars except the rim. The securing of this was for me one of the wonders of the world.

Outside the workshop at ground level was a flat round iron plate large enough to accommodate a cartwheel and with a hole in the centre to receive the hub. It was pivoted over a shallow water-bath. The wooden wheel was laid on the iron plate. Meanwhile, in a high and narrow oven was the iron rim, being evenly heated and expanding as it did so. Then came the exciting part. The rim was pulled from the oven with iron tongs and skilfully dropped over the wooden wheel with just enough clearance all round. Then at the pull of a lever, plate, wheel and rim were submerged in the bath. For a moment the water bubbled and steamed. The iron rim shrank and every joint in the wooden wheel was inexorably squeezed into place, with never a piece of wood splitting.

Next to the wheelwright's shop lay the paint shop. No Aladdin's cave could have boasted a finer entrance. The brickwork on either side of the doorway was no longer discernible, but glistened with paint of every hue. This was the place where paint brushes were cleaned off prior to rinsing in turpentine or immersion in water. For half a century, reds, blues, greens, whites, yellows and a myriad other colours had been wiped onto the brickwork. Colour overlay colour at random. Here and there the very depth of the paint gave an effect that was jewel-like and solid. Ruby, emerald and sapphire shone from a bed of scrambled rainbows. I wondered if tired apprentices had appreciated the effect as I did. The paint shop, some twenty feet square, was lined with shelves which held tins of every shape and size. On some, the label had yellowed and curled, so one could only guess the contents from paint traces on the rim. Some tins were so rusted one wondered if even Zach knew the contents. Clearly labelled were varnishes, wood stains, dyes for colouring whitewash, glue, priming paint, and gloss paint in profusion. Zach was equally at home varnishing a cart or a coffin, painting a farm gate or a house interior, colour-washing a cottage or a church interior. To this day, I can never smell glue without recalling a vision of Zach.

Harold Cramp
(b.1912)

YEOMAN FARMER'S SON

Since most agricultural tenancies end at Michaelmas, September is the busiest month for the auctioneers. It is also the heyday of Henry Higgins. You may meet him anywhere on the road which leads to a sale of furniture or farming stock, and you may recognise him by the legend stencilled neatly on the side of his smart dray: 'MR. H. HIGGINS, BRENSHAM, GNL. DLR.' That 'Mr.' is significant; it is part of his personal dignity, he has a handle to his name! He is proud, independent, individualist; a free man, as he often declares, in a free country. His dignity is implicit too in the shine on his mare's harness and on his own boots and leggings: the sort of shine that is only achieved by elbow-grease. It is as if he were aware that he is certainly the best-known person for twenty miles around, not excluding lords and ladies, and must therefore keep up appearances. Also, there is more to an auction-sale than a bargain and a haggle: it is a minor social occasion, at which a man is liable to encounter a score of old friends. So Mr. Higgins wears his best bowler-hat and a pair of grey breeches rather widely cut out of good cloth by a country tailor who understands the complex sociology of breeches – which have their hierarchies, being shaped with a slight but perceptible difference for various sorts of customers, farmer, vet, dealer, gamekeeper, stable-boy and squire …

I firmly believe that there is nothing in the world he would not buy if he thought the price was right; for his whole life is founded upon a kind of magpie philosophy expressed in four words "It will come in handy." A large orchard behind his house, transformed into a rural slum with fowl-houses, chicken runs, rabbit hutches, pigstyes and sheds, bears witness to the practical application of his philosophy. Piled haphazard in the sheds are iron bedsteads, old chairs, harness, pothampers, odd fragments of broken machinery, cartwheels, implements, drainpipes and sheer junk of every description, all acquired and hoarded on the principle that some day, in circumstances however remote and improbable, these things will come in handy. And sure enough they do. Farmer Dudfield has the misfortune to break some intricate part of the mechanism of his binder at harvest-time, and not even Briggs the blacksmith can fix it; so he takes it along to Mr. Higgins, who stares at it for a long time and 'scrats his yud' and says at last: "I minds I bought an old binder at the Manor Farm sale five years come Michaelmas, and if thee'll help me shift them bits of old bicycles I reckon we'll find her at the back of 'em; and then we'll see if the pieces match up." Or it may be a question of a ball-cock for a cistern when a catastrophe happens to the Rector's plumbing; or a hurricane-lamp or a whetstone or a draining-rod or any of the hundred and one things which feckless countrymen, living far from shops, are apt to need in a hurry. Whatever it is, the chances are that Mr. Higgins will be able to provide it out of his forty years' accumulation if only you give him time to scrat his yud and puzzle out where it may be: which he does by a process of complicated mnemonics: "Now old Matthew Dyer pegged out the day war started; but his sale wasn't till Lady Day. And I bought that pony-trap from a gipsy on the way back from his sale, so if we look behind the pony-trap we ought to come across the horse-clippers I gave a quid for at Matthew Dyer's...

Hardly a day goes by but yields fresh evidence in support of Mr. Higgins's cherished theory about the ultimate handiness of things. Not long ago he bought an ancient Brougham from a man he disliked, who was subsequently very boastful of the fact that he'd got rid of his museum-piece for thirty shillings. But within a few months Mr. Higgins had sold the two front wheels for a pound a piece, and the top for fifteen shillings 'to make a summerhouse' – of all strange improvisations! – and a year later, when the previous owner of the Brougham asked him if he had such a thing as a hand-cart, Mr. Higgins knocked one together out of two packing-cases and fitted it with the rear wheels of the vehicle, for which he took pleasure in charging exactly thirty bob.

John Moore
(1907 - 1967)

COME RAIN, COME SHINE

Arnold drove the bus which crept around our lanes day after day, week after week, to collect passengers at Ashfordly and transport them through the picturesque lanes and villages into York. His bus left Ashfordly at 7.30 a.m. and trundled through Briggsby, Aidensfield, Elsinby, and then beyond the boundaries of my beat and eventually into York. It did a return trip around lunchtime and turned about immediately for York. It arrived in time to turn around in the City at 5.15pm to bring home the diminishing army of workers. Every day, week in week out, Arnold's bus undertook those journeys.

On Tuesdays, Thursdays and Saturdays, he left York immediately upon first arrival and did a special market-day run, collecting at Ashfordly at ten o'clock and getting into York around 11.30 a.m., having done a circuitous tour of Ryedale to get there ...

I learned eventually that Arnold owned the bus. He did not operate for any company, but earned his living entirely by his bus. During the evenings, he would arrange tours to cinemas in York, or to the theatre, and he did runs to the seaside and works outings to breweries and other places of interest. He did a school run too, collecting a rowdy horde of children from isolated places and risking his bus and its passengers on gradients of 1-in-3 as he visited outlying farms and hamlets. But Arnold always got there and very rarely was late. His purple and cream bus, with 'Merryweather Coaches' emblazoned across the rear, was a familiar sight in the hills and valleys of Aidensfield and district.

To fulfil his many commitments, he had two coaches, and had a standby driver employed to assist when necessary. But if it was possible to use one bus and one driver for his complicated timetables then Arnold did so ...

To partake of a trip on Merryweather Coaches was an experience which could be classed as unique. Each bus was identical and I think they were Albion 32-seaters. The seats were made of wooden laths set on iron frames and bolted to the floor. There were no cushions and other comforts, and the door was at the front. It was hinged in the middle and required a good kick from Arnold both to shut it and open it. Arnold acted as driver, conductor and guide as his precious heap of metal navigated the landscape.

My infrequent trips on his coaches proved to be an education. In the few flights I had, I saw him take on board one pig on a halter, three crates of chickens, a sheep and its lamb, a side of ham, several parcels and packages, a bicycle for repair, umpteen suits for cleaning or laundry for washing in York, and on one occasion he transported an unused coffin from Elsinby's undertaker to a man at Ashfordly who wanted it for timber.

These assorted objects were loaded into the bus via the rear emergency door and I learned that Arnold was paid for these sociable services. In addition to being a carrier of people, he was a carrier of objects and this was accepted quite amicably by his human cargo. If Farmer Jones wished to send a pig to Farmer Brown twenty miles away, Arnold would deliver the said animal by bus for a small fee. It seemed a perfectly sound system, but its legality was in grave doubt.

I knew Arnold had been in buses since leaving school and I reckoned he'd put himself on the road long before officials like the Traffic Commissioners appeared with their PSV licences, certifying officers, certificates of fitness and road licences. Nonetheless, he displayed in his wind-screen the various discs which proved someone knew he was operating a bus service. Even so, the other rules and regulations seemed to be superfluous so far as Merryweather's Coaches were concerned.

His transportation of goods for hire or reward, for example, seemed to put him in the category of a goods vehicle rather than a bus, but it would be a stupid constable who attempted to stop that. After all, the fellow had to earn a living and he was doing a service to the community. I knew lots of housebound folks depended upon Arnold for their weekly shopping, for he also spent his non-driving hours in York carrying out shopping requests for pensioners, invalids and others. He dealt with the parcels and packages on his bus, suits for the tailor to repair, carpets for the cleaners to clean, sewing machines to mend, bikes to sell – the whole of society and its well-being made use of Arnold's bus.

Nicholas Rhea
(b.1936)

CONSTABLE AROUND THE VILLAGE

Chapter 5

CREATURES

FOOD

Kate Archy was widow of Fraser, our gardener, and mother of a daughter who succeeded her and remained with the family all her life. I see her now in the high white mutch, herself considerably above ordinary height, stalking over the lawns and along the roads with a strong apron fastened round her, containing, perhaps, seven or eight live chickens, and at her right side a huge pocket. With her right hand she hauls a squalling chicken out of the apron. In a second the left hand holds the feet, the knuckle of the right thumb (did she not teach me herself carefully?) dislocates chicky's neck, and a large handful of feathers goes into the pocket, till in an amazingly short time the featherless victim is thrust away among the survivors in the apron. Then another suddenly goes through the same ceremony, till all are served. When Kate's walk round the place ends in the kitchen of the Tigh Dige seven or eight chickens, merely needing 'flamming,' are lying on the table for the housekeeper's orders. And don't I remember her sometimes allowing me, as a reward for being good, to flam the feather-plucked flesh, passing the bird suddenly through the flames of some paper, which burnt off all the small feathers or down?

Osgood MacKenzie
(1842 – 1922)

100 Years in the Highlands

The whole scene, with its mud and blood, flaring lights and dark shadows, was as savage as anything to be seen in an African jungle. The children at the end house would steal out of bed to the window. 'Look! Look! It's hell, and those are the devils,' Edmund would whisper, pointing to the men tossing the burning straw with their pitchforks; but Laura felt sick and would creep back into bed and cry: she was sorry for the pig.

But, hidden from the children, there was another aspect of the pig killing. Months of hard work and self denial were brought on that night to a successful conclusion. It was time to rejoice, and rejoice they did with beer flowing freely and the first delicious dish of pig's fry sizzling in the frying pan.

The next day, when the carcass had been cut up, joints of pork were distributed to those neighbours who had sent similar ones at their own pig killing. Small plates of fry and other oddments were sent to others as a pure compliment, and no one who happened to be ill or down on his luck at these occasions was ever forgotten.

Then the housewife 'got down to it', as she said. Hams and sides of bacon were salted, to be taken out of the brine later and hung on the wall near the fireplace to dry. Lard was dried out, hogs' puddings were made, and the chitterlings were cleaned and turned three days in succession under running water, according to ancient ritual. It was a busy time, but a happy one, with the larder full and something over to give away, and all the pride and importance of owning such riches.

On the following Sunday came the official 'pig feast', when fathers and mothers, sisters and brothers, married children and grandchildren who lived within walking distance arrived to dinner.

If the house had no oven, permission was obtained from the old couple in one of the thatched cottages to heat up the big bread-baking oven in their wash-house. This was like a large cupboard with an iron door, lined with brick and going far back into the wall. Faggots of wood were lighted inside and the door was closed upon them until the oven was well heated. Then the ashes were swept out on baking-tins with joints of pork, potatoes, batter puddings, pork pies, and sometimes a cake or two, were popped inside and left to bake without further attention.

Meanwhile, at home, three or four different kinds of vegetables would be cooked, and always a meat pudding, made in a basin. No feast and few Sunday dinners were considered complete without that item, which was eaten alone, without vegetables, when a joint was to follow. On ordinary days the pudding would be a roly-poly containing fruit, currants or jam; but it still appeared as a first course, the idea being that it took the edge off the appetite.

At the big feast there would be no sweet pudding, for that could be had any day, and who wanted sweet things when there was plenty of meat to be had!

Flora Thompson
(1867 – 1947)

LARK RISE TO CANDLEFORD

'Not long ago, Flavell, the Methodist preacher was brought up for knocking down a hare that came across his path when he and his wife were walking out together. He was pretty quick, and knocked it on the neck.' 'That was very brutal, I think,' said Dorothea.

'Well, now, it seemed rather black to me, I confess, in a Methodist preacher, you know. And Johnson said, 'You may judge what a hypocrite he is.' And upon my word, I thought

Flavell looked very little like 'the highest style of man' – as somebody calls the Christian – Young, the poet Young, I think – you know Young? Well, now, Flavell in his shabby black gaiters, pleading that he thought the Lord had sent him and his wife a good dinner, and he had a right to knock it down, though not a mighty hunter before the Lord, as Nimrod was – I assure you it was rather comic: Fielding would have made something of it – or Scott, now – Scott might have worked it up. But really, when I came to think of it, I couldn't help liking that the fellow should have a bit of hare to say grace over. It's all a matter of prejudice – prejudice with the law on its side, you know – about the stick and the gaiters, and so on. However, it doesn't do to reason about things; and law is law. But I got Johnson to be quiet, and I hushed the matter up.

George Eliot
(1819 - 1880)

MIDDLEMARCH

CONTROL

I think that he fixed himself the more firmly in my memory by his singular discrepancy with the beauty and cheerfulness of the scenery and the season. Isaac is a tall, lean, gloomy personage; with whom the clock of life seems to stand still. He has looked sixty-five for these last twenty years, although his dark hair and beard, and firm manly stride, almost contradict the evidence of his sunken cheeks and deeply lined forehead. The stride is awful: he hath the stalk of a ghost. His whole air and demeanour savour of one that comes from underground. His appearance is "of the earth, earthy". His clothes, hands, and face are of the colour of the mould in which he delves. The little round traps which hang behind him over one shoulder, as well as the strings of dead moles which embellish the other, are encrusted with dirt like a tombstone; and the staff which he plunges into the little hillocks, by which he traces the course of his small quarry, returns a hollow sound, as if tapping on the lid of a coffin. Images of the churchyard come, one does not know how, with his presence. Indeed he does officiate as assistant to the sexton in his capacity of grave-digger, chosen as it should seem, from a natural fitness; a fine sense of congruity in good Joseph Reed, the functionary in question, who felt, without knowing why, that, of all men in the parish, Isaac Bint was best fitted to that solemn office.

Mary Russell Mitford
(1787 – 1855)

English Life and Character

There is another character in the village who deserves mention, Brickett my keeper.

When I took a small shoot in the locality, principally to help out with the rationing, for there is nothing on it save multitudes of rabbits, I cast around for a man to look after it for me. Brickett was recommended and I took him on. He had been a keeper on a big estate and is quite one of the old school. He is a typical keeper in appearance, of middle height with what I call a fiery face and a truculent blue eye. He wears a wide skirted coat of antique cut with big hare pockets. This coat belongs to his earlier life, of big woods, pheasant pens and winter shoots, a life which is fast disappearing. He pursues the so-called 'sport' of rabbit catching with a peculiar intensity and perseverance, reminding me of a terrier.

He has three ferrets, all extremely bad workers, but he looks after them well and feeds them regularly; some say he thinks more of his ferrets than he does of his wife, indeed it is whispered in the village that he beats his wife on occasion, but only in his cups.

I shot a good many rabbits early on in the season by walking round, but now there is not cover in the hedges and none on the fields, so Brickett has to ferret them, a 'sport' I loathe for it is a cad's sport. Yet it is the only way to get these rabbits out. The largest warren, Crow Wood, is a steep bank which was once the site of an ancient monastery. The bank is honeycombed with holes all along its length and once a ferret gets in these burrows it is gone for hours.

The most usual view I have of Brickett is a stern view, with his head down a hole calling to his ferret or listening for a rabbit. Now matter how cold the wind he grubs among the red earth, his hands caked with it, impervious to frost, as keen and hard as an old lurcher.

He ties sacking round his knees for 'kneelers', he never wears a top coat, though in really wet weather he dons a tattered 'mac'. His ferrets never bite him (at least so he says) because he feeds them 'in the dark'.

He remembers fights with poachers in the old days and how one moonlight night, by the big plantation, he and his father who was the head-keeper, and another under-keeper, set about a gang of roughs who were after the pheasants. He was only a lad and soon got knocked out. He rolled into the ditch and lay there trembling. He saw a big man go for his father with the stock of a gun, but down came the good old ash plant on the fellow's head.

'Lor bless you sir it wur a tarrible blow me father give 'im, the chap just crumpled up on the ground with his 'ead split open. I knew me father 'ad 'it too 'ard, but if 'e 'adnt, it would 'ave bin 'im that 'ad the cracked skull. The man was dead sure enough with 'is skull stove in, same as an egg shell.'

'B.B.' (Denys Watkins-Pitchford)
(1905 – 1990)

COUNTRYMAN'S BEDSIDE BOOK

SPORT

Looking hard at the distance, George Purse saw the first covey come sweeping over the ridge, a few feet above the heather. He glanced at Lord Dronfield, but he had seen them at the same time. He stiffened slightly, stood a little straighter and leaned forward. At the first sight of the game that aloof, slightly ponderous elderly gentleman had suddenly focused into a harder, sharper man.

In case any of the grouse decided to sheer off at any sudden movement in the butts, or looked like missing the butts altogether and escaping down the sides, a line of men had been positioned at an angle on both flanks. Their job was to pop up from the heather and wave their flags, in an attempt to scare the deviants back into the line of fire.

But there were no deviants in this covey, which formed the vanguard of the birds in flight from the beaters. They were heading straight towards the middle of the line of butts, trying to escape over the top of the butts, where eight double barrelled shotguns were waiting to receive them, with another eight in reserve when those had discharged. Straight forward, head on; it was now possible to see the downward curved silhouette of their wings as they glided, the way their bodies rocked from side to side when they flew.

Forty yards out, thirty, Lord Dronfield mounted his gun and fired. He missed, the bird jinked, second barrel, same bird, a puff of feathers and the grouse collapsed in front of the butt. He passed the gun back, the gamekeeper took it, pushed forward the second gun and rapidly reloaded the first. Guns to the right and guns to the left were also firing. Grouse which remained untouched by the swarms of lead pellets zinging out towards them were still not safe. The Guns waited until they had passed between the butts, then shot at them as they flew away.

Grouse were arriving frequently now, not in great flocks which darkened the sky and allowed all the Guns to blaze away simultaneously, but in families, and pairs and odd penny numbers presenting themselves at different places along the line so that the Guns were kept busy, but not overworked.

George Purse was bristling with cartridges. They were stuck between his fingers and there were two clenched in his teeth. He had to be quick now, the birds were coming in fast. Right barrel, left barrel, pass back, hand forward. He broke the breech, the cartridge cases ejected automatically and there was the reek of powder from the barrels. He inserted two fresh cartridges and closed the gun to reload and pass it back. They handled the guns smoothly, there was no fumbling between them, and when they exchanged guns, their barrels were always pointing skywards for safety. In the confined space of that hot little fortress, George Purse served his Gun expertly. Lord Dronfield never had to think about him. All he did was pull both triggers, hand back the gun and another took its place. Sometimes a quiet voice said, 'on your left, sir', and there it was, on his left, or, 'a brace on your right, sir', and there was a brace on his right. When Lord Dronfield swivelled to take a bird behind, George Purse always anticipated the move and ducked early, to give him an unobstructed shot. Besides loading, and looking for the grouse he also had to remember where they fell so that he would know where to direct his dogs when the drive was over.

Shooting etiquette between the Guns was strict. They only shot the birds in the area before or behind their own butts. If there was any doubt whose bird it was, they called to establish rights, and they never shot at birds passing between the butts in case they hit someone in a butt further up the line.

Then they were all gone. The last gunshot reverberated around the hills, and the line of beaters came walking over the ridge, waving their white flags. The shooting party watched them, guns ready, should anything get up between them. But nothing flew, all the grouse were either dead, wounded, or had temporarily escaped to the other side of the moor. Two hundred yards from the butts the beaters stopped and lowered their flags, and for a few seconds the Guns and the beaters faced each other in silence. The moor was quiet again, and larks and meadow pipits started to re-assert themselves in the temporary peace.

Barry Hines
(b. 1939)

THE GAMEKEEPER

Ringwell cubbing days are among my happiest memories. Those mornings now reappear in my mind, lively and freshly painted by the sunshine of an autumn that made amends for the rainy weeks which had washed away the summer. Four days a week we were up before daylight. I had heard the snoring stable-hands roll out of bed with yawns and grumblings, and they were out and about before the reticent Henry came into my room with a candle and a jug of warm water. (How Henry managed to get up was a mystery.) Any old clothes were good enough for cubbing, and I was very soon downstairs in the stuffy little living-room, where Denis had an apparatus for boiling eggs. While they were bubbling he put the cocoa-powder in the cups, two careful spoonfuls each, and not a grain more. A third spoonful was unthinkable.

Not many minutes afterwards we were out by the range of loose boxes under the rustling trees, with quiet stars overhead and scarcely a hint of morning. In the kennels the two packs were baying at one another from their separate yards, and as

soon as Denis had got his horse from the gruff white-coated head-groom, a gate released the hounds — twenty-five or thirty couple of them, and all very much on their toes. Out they streamed like a flood of water, throwing their tongues and spreading away in all directions wlth waving sterns, as though they had never been out in the world before. Even then I used to feel the strangeness of the scene with its sharp exuberance of unkennelled energy. Will's hearty voice and the crack of his whip stood out above the clamour and commotion which surged around Denis and his horse. Then, without any apparent lull or interruption, the whirlpool became a well-regulated torrent flowing through the gateway into the road, along which the sound of hoofs receded with a purposeful clip-clopping. Whereupon I hoisted myself on to an unknown horse – usually an excited one – and set off higgledy-piggledy along the road to catch them up. Sometimes we had as many as twelve miles to go, but more often we were at the meet in less than an hour.

The mornings I remember most zestfully were those which took us up on to the chalk downs. To watch the day breaking from purple to dazzling gold while we trotted up a deep-rutted lane; to inhale the early freshness when we were on the sheep-cropped uplands; to stare back at the low country with its cock-crowing farms and mist-coiled waterways; thus to be riding out with a sense of spacious discovery – was it not something stolen from the lie-a-bed world and the luckless city workers – even though it ended in nothing more than the killing of a leash of fox cubs? (for whom, to tell the truth, I felt an unconfessed sympathy). Up on the downs in fine September weather sixteen years ago ...

It is possible that even then, if I was on a well-behaved horse, I could half forget why we were there, so pleasant was it to be alive and gazing around me. But I would be dragged out of my day dream by Denis when he shouted to me to wake up and get round to the far side of the covert; for on such hill days we often went straight to one of the big gorses without any formality of a meet. There were beech woods, too, in the folds of the downs, and lovely they looked in the mellow sunshine, with summer's foliage falling in ever-deepening drifts among their gnarled and mossy roots.

Siegfried Sassoon
(1886 – 1967)

Memoirs of a Fox-Hunting Man

I have an old book by a Salisbury resident, William Chafin, an account of a bustard hunt in the year 1751. It took place on the downs near Winterslow Hut, now the Pheasant Inn, and Chafin describes how he went out after partridges and green plover, and also a small flock of dotterel, which are a species I have never seen in southern England. Presently he secured a shot and:

'On the report of my gun, on the further end of the field, about a quarter of a mile from me, twenty-five bustards got up and flew very quietly over the hill called Southern Hill. Before I went in pursuit of such noble game I thought it proper to take my dogs to the inn, and confine them there ...

'Then I drew the charge of small shot from my gun, and supplied its place with swan shot, which I always carried with me for such an occasion; and, having put a new flint in my gun, mounted my horse and went in pursuit of the bustards; but my mind misgave me at the time, that it would turn out a mere wild-goose chase. When I came to the brow of the hill over which I had seen them pass, I rode very cautiously, looking carefully before me, when on a sudden I espied them within shot, and they espied me also, and rose for flight.

'The motion of their wings frightened my horse; he started back, threw me down and ran away. As soon as I got upon my knees, I fired at the birds, but without effect. After they had taken their flight over the opposite hill all together, I saw one of them return and alight on the side of it, and spread out one of his wings as if wounded. I had no doubt that it was so, and made sure that I should have him. I therefore charged my gun hastily, and made my way towards him in the most cautious manner I could; but before I could come within shot, he took flight and followed the same line in which his companions had flown. I conjectured, therefore, that he had been dispatched as a sentinel or spy, to watch my motions. Thus disappointed, I made the best of my way home, about three miles, chagrined and tired.'

Ralph Whitlock
(1914 – 1995)

A FAMILY AND A VILLAGE

WORK

The tractors lie about our fields; at evening
They look like dank sea-monsters couched and waiting.
We leave them where they are and let them rust:
'They'll moulder away and be like other loam'.
We make our oxen drag our rusty ploughs,
Long laid aside. We have gone back
Far past our father's land.
                              And then, that evening
Late in the summer the strange horses came.
We heard a distant tapping on the road,
A deepening drumming; it stopped, went on again
And at the corner changed to hollow thunder.
We saw the heads
Like a wild wave charging and were afraid.
We had sold our horses in our fathers' time
To buy new tractors. Now they were strange to us
As fabulous steeds set on an ancient shield
Or illustrations in a book of knights.
We did not dare go near them. Yet they waited,
Stubborn and shy, as if they had been sent
By an old command to find our whereabouts
And that long-lost archaic companionship.

In the first moment we had never thought
That they were creatures to be owned and used.
Among them were some half-a-dozen colts
Dropped in some wilderness of the broken world,
Yet new as if they had come from their own Eden.
Since then they have pulled our ploughs and borne
our loads
But that free servitude still can pierce our hearts.
Our life is changed; their coming our beginning.

Edwin Muir
(1887 – 1959)

from *The Horses*

Throughout the summer months, many sheepmen participate in the increasingly popular pastime of sheepdog trialling. The very first trials were held in 1873 to promote, of all things, the sale of Welsh whisky.

On the third Saturday of this month, the local trials are held at the Garrison of Inversnaid. I have entered with Mona, and we have been drawn to run somewhere around mid-afternoon, the order of trial having been decided by ballot. We arrive *en famille* at the trial field soon after lunch. I report my presence to the secretary and enquire after the leading points of the dogs already run.

At my post, I position Mona on my left-hand side, the side I intend to run her. As soon as my sheep are in a good position I send Mona on her way. She runs rather wide at the start, skirting a dense stand of bracken, and no doubt the judge will have a bit off for that. Mona moves in nicely behind her sheep and lies down. The sheep stand still. I whistle her up to lift them. And again. Jimmy Shanks will have pencilled off another point or two.

The fetch could not be much straighter, the bare hoggs coming on smoothly. As they approach my post, I back away a little so that Mona can keep her charges in as direct a line as possible. She turns them round the post in a clockwise direction and begins her drive. Here we meet our first real problem. The ground between me and the first set of drive gates is extremely soggy. Rather than take a drier detour and lose points, we persevere on the direct path, and lose a lot of precious time. At long last we get out of the bog and through the gate. I give a bye command to turn the sheep onto the cross drive, and we are under way once more. A slight waver at the second set of hurdles allows one hogg to slip past on the wrong side. More points gone. Mona brings the sheep around towards the pen.

I can leave my post now, and go over to the pen. With the gate wide open, Mona comes up on her sheep: close … closer, the sheep shuffle about nervously. One breaks away. Mona flanks in a flash of black and white, turns the beast back to the rest. Up again, steady … and they are in. I shut the gate and heave a sigh of relief. Out again, quickly. Time must be getting short. But before we can steady the flying hoggs and attempt a shed, the dreaded whistle sounds out for time up. Nevertheless, I am well pleased. That was a good enough run to put us well up in the prize list – at the moment. Whether I stay there depends upon the work that follows.

John Barrington
(b. 1945)

Red Sky At Night

The Ploughman's Horse

Sweet then the ploughman's slumbers, hale and young,
When the last topic dies upon his tongue;
Sweet then the bliss his transient dreams inspire,
Till chilblains wake him, or the snapping fire.
He starts, and ever thoughtful of his team,
Along the glittering snow a feeble gleam
Shoots from his lantern, as he yawning goes
To add fresh comforts to their night's repose;
Diffusing fragrance as their food he moves,
And pats the jolly sides of those he loves.
Thus full replenished, perfect ease possessed,
From night till morn alternate food and rest,
No rightful cheer withheld, no sleep debarred,
Their each day's labour brings its sure reward.
Yet when from plough or lumbering cart set free,
They taste a while the sweets of liberty:
E'en sober Dobbin lifts his clumsy heel
And kicks, disdainful of the dirty wheel;
But soon, his frolic ended, yields again
To trudge the road, and wear the clinking chain.

Robert Bloomfield
(1766 – 1823)
from *Winter*

OBSERVATION

Knowing when and where to look for a thing was one of his gifts. Walking through a wood on a bleak March day, I would see nothing but coarse, brown bracken, but he would search beneath the undergrowth and show me tender green fronds, or the first fresh spikes of a bluebell pushing through the carpet of moss. When the birds had mated, he would lift the very branch of a fir tree from which the fragile nest of a goldcrest was suspended, or walk straight to a furze bush and disclose the speckled pale blue eggs of a linnet. He had only to turn his head to see something of interest. It was almost uncanny the way he sensed things. Stirrings in a tuft of grass I naturally thought were caused by the breeze, but he knew better, and he would find a shrew mouse lurking beneath it. He would notice a branch swinging slightly out of rhythm with its neighbours, and, sure enough, a linnet would be swaying on it. Sometimes he called Raq to heel unnecessarily, I thought, but a few paces ahead he would show me the gamekeeper's deadly trap hidden from view in the brushwood. A sudden change in the direction of a bird's flight would convey nothing to me, but to him it meant danger, and he would run ahead just in time to see a fox slinking up a hedgeside. There never seemed a time of year when he could not find something. To him this was life, and what he had left behind in the town, an existence.

Eunice Evens (Mrs. George Bramwell Evens)
(1885 – 1943)

THROUGH THE YEARS WITH ROMANY

March Hares

I made myself as a tree,
No withered leaf twirling on me;
No, not a bird that stirred my boughs,
As looking out from wizard brows
I watched those lithe and lovely forms
That raised the leaves in storms.

I watched them leap and run,
Their bodies hollowed in the sun
To thin transparency,
That I could clearly see
The shallow colour of their blood
Joyous in love's full flood.

I was content enough
Watching that serious game of love,
That happy hunting in the wood
Where the pursuer was the more pursued,
To stand in breathless hush
With no more life myself than tree or bush.

Andrew Young
(1885 - 1971)

Country People

CARE

Tom Merlin, even in the sternest conflict in the market, always kept his temper. Only once was he known to lose it, at any rate, in public. That was when he found a heavy-handed lout of a labourer beating a sheep-dog with a great ash stick. It was late one market day, and the dog was tied to a pen in the cattle market. The wretched creature was half strangled in its efforts to get away from its tormentor.

Tom strode over to the fellow with the ash plant.

'That'll do,' he said. 'Tha's done plenty to t'poor beast. Give ower now.'

'Mind thi own blasted business,' said the man, and brought down the ash plant again.

'Stop it, I tell thee,' said Tom. 'If tha hits that dog again, I'll kill thee.'

It was unfortunate for the man that he ignored the threat, though fortunate that the onlookers dragged Tom away after he had only hit him twice. It was several weeks before the lout with the ash plant lost the marks of Tom's anger.

'Nay, I made a gurt fooil o' missen,' said Tom to himself later that day as he pulled out his tin whistle and piped himself into a better frame of mind. 'Mi old Dad would a'bin capped if he'd know Tom Boy 'ud lost his temper ower nobbut a dog.'

Richard Harman

COUNTRYSIDE CHARACTER

'I don't see how you can create a habitat and encourage the birds to nest and not try to control the vermin,' Bernard Bishop said. 'I'm not saying you should kill the last one, but they have to be controlled.'

Bernard Bishop still lives in Watcher's Cottage where he was born. Bernard Bishop's father, Billy, had been an expert, with an unrivalled eye and 'feel for birds'; he had been a colourful character whose wisdom and no-nonsense approach were relished by all those who knew him, and the improvements he carried out to the marsh attracted three rarities back to the area, the avocets, the bearded reedlings and the bitterns. Now the Cley Marsh Reserve has one of the largest colonies of avocets breeding in this country.

'I used to go out on the reserve with my father and help him,' Bernard said. 'It was a lovely childhood.'

Sitting at the kitchen table, drinking tea with Bernard Bishop we looked out over the reserve.

'It is never the same twice,' he said. 'You get different lights on the reeds all the time and the water-levels change all through the winter. In winter I feel as if the marsh belongs to me. We start cutting the reeds just before Christmas and sell them to the thatchers. Those reeds are a beautiful green in summer and then when the leaves come off they turn a lovely, golden colour.'

'We get mostly migratory waders here,' Bernard Bishop said. 'We get long-legged birds like sandpipers, red-shanks, green-shanks and various stints, and we get the occasional surprise. Last year a little whimbrel turned up. They're supposed to migrate from Japan to Australia so I don't know what it was doing here. We had a Rosser's gull too, from the Arctic Circle – a beautiful rose-pink gull. That was a rarity. In March you get the birds nesting – bitterns, bearded reedlings and last year we had 54 pairs of avocets.'

Josephine Haworth
(b.1934)

The Country Habit

Mrs Pumphrey received me with a joyful cry. 'Oh, Mr Herriot, isn't it wonderful! I have the most darling little pig. I was visiting some cousins who are farmers and I picked him out. He will be such company for Tricki – you know how I worry about his being an only dog.'

I shook my head vigorously in bewilderment as I crossed the oak-panelled hall. My visits here were usually associated with a degree of fantasy but I was beginning to feel out of my depth.

'You mean you actually have this pig in the house?'

'But of course.' Mrs Pumphrey looked surprised. 'He's in the kitchen. Come and see him.'

I had been in this kitchen a few times and had been almost awestruck by its shining spotlessness; the laboratory look of the tiled walls and floors, the gleaming surfaces of sink unit, cooker, refrigerator. Today, a cardboard box occupied one corner and inside I could see a tiny pig; standing on his hind legs, his fore-feet resting on the rim, he was looking round him appreciatively at his new surroundings.

The elderly cook had her back to us and did not look round when we entered; she was chopping carrots and hurling them into a saucepan with, I thought, unnecessary vigour.

'Isn't he adorable!' Mrs Pumphrey bent over and tickled the little head. 'It is so exciting having a pig of my very own! Mr Herriot, I have decided to call him Nugent.'

I swallowed. 'Nugent?' The cook's broad back froze into immobility.

'Yes, after my great uncle Nugent. He was a little pink man with tiny eyes and a snub nose. The resemblance is striking.'

'I see,' I said, and the cook started her splashing again.

For a few moments I was at a loss; the ethical professional man in me rebelled at the absurdity of examining this obviously healthy little creature. In fact I was on the point of saying that he looked perfectly all right to me when Mrs Pumphrey spoke.

'Come now, Nugent,' she said. 'You must be a good boy and let your Uncle Herriot look at you.'

That did it. Stifling my finer feelings I seized the string like tail and held Nugent almost upside down as I took his temperature. I then solemnly auscultated his heart and lungs, peered into his eyes, ran my fingers over his limbs and flexed his joints...

The examination over, I turned to Mrs Pumphrey who was anxiously awaiting the verdict. 'Sound in all respects,' I said briskly. 'In fact you've got a very fine pig there. But there's just one thing – he can't live in the house.'

For the first time the cook turned towards me and I read a mute appeal in her face. I could sympathize with her because the excretions of the pig are peculiarly volatile and even such a minute specimen as Nugent had already added his own faint pungency to the atmosphere in the kitchen.

Mrs Pumphrey was appalled at the idea at first but when I assured her that he wouldn't catch pneumonia and in fact would be happier and healthier outside, she gave way. An agricultural joiner was employed to build a palatial sty in a corner of the garden; it had a warm sleeping apartment on raised boards and an outside run. I saw Nugent installed in it, curled blissfully in a bed of clean straw. His trough was filled twice daily with the best meal and he was never short of an extra titbit such as a juicy carrot or some cabbage leaves. In short, Nugent had it made, but it couldn't have happened to a nicer pig; because,

though most of his species have an unsuspected strain of friendliness, this was developed in Nugent to an extraordinary degree. He just liked people and over the next few months his character flowered under the constant personal contact with humans.

Nugent's existence was sunny and there was only one cloud in the sky; old Hodgkin, the gardener, whose attitude to domestic pets had been permanently soured by having to throw rubber rings for Tricki every day, now found himself appointed personal valet to a pig. It was his duty to feed and bed down Nugent and to supervise his play periods. The idea of doing all this for a pig who was never going to be converted into pork pies must have been nearly insupportable for the old countryman; the harsh lines on his face deepened whenever he took hold of the meal bucket.

James Herriot
(1916 – 1995)

IT SHOULDN'T HAPPEN TO A VET

The vet was lean, angular, and humorous in a reserved way. He wore a check cap, a longish riding-coat that splayed out at the hips, and tight-fitting leggings.

He was about all hours, all days, all weathers. If anything, he seemed a little busier on Sundays (which, as every farmer knows, is the one day for any untoward events on a farm – milk fevers, mating-fevers, breaking out of pigs, etc.) But that he was conscious of the day was evident by the fact that he always wore a bowler hat and long trousers then, though they must have incommoded him in his work. It seemed a sign that he always got up quite prepared to spend Sunday as a day of rest, for all that by nine-thirty or so there would come a call for him, and by the time he had returned, two or three more had probably accumulated. He always seemed quite happy about it.

'Don't you ever get a Sunday off?' asked my mother.

He shrugged. 'I don't mind. You see, I am fond of my work. Though you get some funny jobs sometimes. It's not a bit of use anybody taking it up unless they love the work. An animal's not like a human being – it can't speak – it can't tell you where it's got a pain – you've got to find out; so you've got to understand it – you've got to have a lot of patience.'

His own patience was inspiring. I have seen him faced with a colt that had torn its side on a stake, one that had never had a halter on its head till half Mr. Colville's men had managed to catch it and bring it kicking and rearing into the yard for treatment. He coaxed, lightly touching, patting, stroking, and then dodged the creature's heels as it let fly.

In frosty dead of night, by dim lantern light misted with our breath, I have stooped with him over a horse whose glazed eyes looked up at us between life and death. Or it has been a Sunday afternoon, with Benfield bells ringing to church, when he has hung his bowler on a peg in the cow-shed, and his coat, and rolled up his shirt-sleeves, and set about some midwifery. And so he went his way, and still goes – week by week – by night as by day – with barns for sick-rooms, straw for an operating table, and yokels for nurses. Good luck to him.

Adrian Bell
1902 - 1983)

Silver Ley

COMMUNICATION

Once, on the rocks off Rhu Arisaig, I picked up a brown seal pup no more than a day or so old – he had the soft white baby coat that is more often shed in the womb, and he seemed for all the world like a toy designed to please a child. He was warm and tubby and not only unafraid but squirmingly affectionate, and I set him down again with some reluctance. But he was not to be so easily left, for as I moved off he came shuffling and humping along at my heels. After a few minutes of trying to shake him off I tried dodging and hiding behind rocks, but he discovered me with amazing agility. Finally I scrambled down to the boat and rowed quickly away, but after twenty yards he was there beside me muzzling an oar. I was in desperation to know what to do with this unexpected foundling whose frantic mother was now snorting twenty yards away, when suddenly he responded to one of her calls and the two went off together, the pup no doubt to receive the lecture of his life.

Gavin Maxwell

(1914 – 1969)

RING OF BRIGHT WATER

Whenever an order for a coffin came, Hazel went to tell the bees who was dead. Her father thought this unnecessary. It was only for folks that died in the house, he said. But he had himself told the bees when his wife died. He had gone out on that vivid June morning to his hives, and had stood watching the lines of bees fetching water, their shadows going and coming on the clean white boards. Then he had stooped and said with a curious confidential indifference, 'Maray's jead.' He had put his ear to the hive and listened to the deep, solemn murmur within; but it was the murmur of the future, and not of the past, the preoccupation with life, not with death, that filled the pale galleries within. To-day the eighteen hives lay under their winter covering, and the eager creatures within slept. Only one or two strayed sometimes to the early arabis, desultory and sad, driven home again by the frosty air to await the purple times of honey.

The happiest days of Abel's life were those when he sat like a bard before the seething hives and harped to the muffled roar of sound that came from within.

Mary Webb
(1881 - 1929)

Gone to Earth

Saint Brendan, too, discovered an island Paradise of Birds. Their singing was 'like the music of heaven'. The saint conversed with their spokesman and was informed that at one time they had all been angels but when Lucifer fell they were brought down with him. Their offence being trivial, they were permitted to make merry in their tree. Brendan and his companions kept Easter there and remained until after Whitsuntide 'and the birds sang Matins and verses of the psalms, and sang all the Hours as is the habit of Christian men.'

Edward Armstrong

St. Francis' Nature Mysticism

But the birds don't come to us solely for food. Sometimes they come just to be friendly. The kitchen door is normally wide open, except during the cold and wet weather, and in order to keep out any wandering mouse the doorway is guarded at the base by a 9-inch-high piece of wood. Scrit, our blackbird, likes to sit upon this piece of wood and sing quiet little sub-songs. He will sit there singing to himself quite happily so long as I am clattering about in the kitchen. If I stop working, or go and speak to him, he will instantly stop singing and look self-conscious. Sometimes, on these occasions, I toss him a scrap of food. He looks down at it with one eye, half-heartedly, and more often than not he will ignore it and carry on warbling to himself as soon as my back is turned.

When Alan is working around the garden he will always have a personal attendant of some bird or another. I once went to look for him and found him sitting happily in the privy, the door open to the sunshine and the view. With his trousers around his ankles he was enjoying a quiet smoke. A few inches further along the pine-wood seat sat an equally contented looking blue tit ... Chaffinches are also fond of him. He had an affair with a female chaffinch (known as Miss Chee) which lasted for several years. She used to follow him around. One day he spent some hours shifting a load of coal that had been dumped in the field. With his wheelbarrow he trudged back and forth between the field and the chicken house (where we kept the coal then). Walking behind him – a few feet away – was Miss Chee. Hopping over the tussocks of grass, walking daintily where the grass was short, she trailed behind him like a little shadow all morning.

We seem to communicate with our birds on two levels. There is the chatty, cheerful level with the birds we know personally; they can tell what we are thinking because of the tone of our voices and our actions. In the same way we are able to know what they want. But there is also a deeper, more urgent, form of communication, usually in times of distress, and quite often with birds that would normally keep their distance from us. One year the pair of swallows that were nesting in the stable came to the cottage door. They hovered in the doorway chittering with anxiety, then flew back to the stable. Within seconds they were back again, hovering and crying. The message was loud and clear. Please come and help! We raced along to the stable, and found a cat standing on top of one of the wooden partitions, almost within a paw's reach of the nest of youngsters peering anxiously over the edge. On another occasion Alan was able to communicate to a frightened robin a sensible course of action. The Hafod robins are now happy, friendly little chaps, but in the early days they were very timid. This particular robin (called Isaac) flew into the kitchen by accident one day. Panic-stricken, he fluttered first of all at the kitchen window, and then shot up the stairs. He flew crazily around a large cupboard off the landing when Alan went up, and he battered himself against the skylight in a frenzy. Alan walked across to Isaac, holding out his hand, and saying 'Come on, robin'. He said he felt strongly that the robin must sit upon his hand. And he did. He stayed absolutely still as Alan approached with an outstretched hand until his fingers were at his breast; then Isaac lightly stepped on. Alan carried him to the window in the nearest bedroom, opened it, and a very frightened Isaac was free.

Elizabeth West

(b.1932)

GARDEN IN THE HILLS

COMPANIONSHIP

Tammy was a trotter, at one time known all over the county, for he won every trotting race for which he was entered, except one, in which he finished second because of a bad handicap. Tammy will never be sold or allowed to suffer. One of Tammy's greatest deeds was done when grandfather fell from the spring cart and lay on the frozen road until someone came and lifted him from between his horse's forefeet. Until help came Tammy licked his master's face and obeyed his instructions to stand still on the brow of a slippery hill.

John McNeellie

The Countryman, Summer, 1935

Johnny always made me feel better because he was invariably optimistic and wore a cheerful grin which never altered, even though he was blind. He was about my own age and he sat there in his habitual pose, one hand on the head of his guide dog, Fergus.

'Is it inspection time again already, Johnny?' I asked.

'Aye, it is that, Mr Herriot, it's come round again. It's been a quick six months.' He laughed and held out his card. I squatted and looked into the face of the big Alsatian sitting motionless and dignified by his master's side.

'Well, and how's Fergus these days7'

'Oh he's in grand fettle. Eatin' well and full of life.' The hand on the head moved round to the ears and at the other end the tail did a bit of sweeping along the waiting-room floor.

As I looked at the young man, his face alight with pride and affection, I realised afresh what this dog meant to him. He had told me that when his failing sight progressed to total blindness in his early twenties he was filled with a despair which did not lessen until he was sent to train with a guide dog and met Fergus; because he found something more than another living creature to act as his eyes, he found a friend and companion to share every moment of his days.

'Well, we'd better get started,' I said. 'Stand up a minute, old lad, while I take your temperature.' That was normal and I went over the big animal's chest with a stethoscope, listening to the reassuringly steady thud of the heart. As I parted the long hair along the neck and back to examine the skin I laughed.

'I'm wasting my time here, Johnny. You've got his coat in perfect condition.'

'Aye, never a day goes by but he gets a good groomin'.'

I had seen him at it, brushing and combing tirelessly to bring extra lustre to the sleek swathes of hair. The nicest thing anybody could say to Johnny was, 'That's a beautiful dog you've got.' His pride in that beauty was boundless even though he had never seen it himself.

Treating guide dogs for the blind has always seemed to me to be one of a veterinary surgeon's most rewarding tasks. To be in a position to help and care for these magnificent animals is a privilege, not just because they are highly trained and valuable but because they represent in the ultimate way some thing which has always lain near the core and centre of my life: the mutually depending, trusting and loving association between man and animal.

Meeting these blind people was a humbling experience which sent me about my work with a new appreciation of my blessings.

I opened the dog's mouth and peered at the huge gleaming teeth. It was dicing with danger to do this with some Alsatians, but with Fergus you could haul the great jaws apart and nearly put your head in and he would only lick your ear. In fact he was at it now. My cheek was nicely within range and he gave it a quick wipe with his large wet tongue.

'Hey, just a minute, Fergus!' I withdrew and plied my handkerchief. 'I've had a wash this morning. And anyway, only little dogs lick – not big tough Alsatians.'

Johnny threw back his head and gave a great peal of laughter. 'There's nowt tough about him, he's the softest dog you could ever meet.'

James Herriot
(1916 – 1995)

VETS MIGHT FLY

His daily life was of a curious microscopic sort, his whole world being limited to a circuit of a few feet from his person. His familiars were creeping and winged things, and they seemed to enrol him in their band. Bees hummed around his ears with an intimate air, and tugged at the heath and furze-flowers at his side in such numbers as to weigh them down to the sod. The strange amber-coloured butterflies which Egdon produced, and which were never seen elsewhere, quivered in the breath of his lips, alighted upon his bowed back, and sported with the glittering point of his hook as he flourished it up and down. Tribes of emerald-green grasshoppers leaped over his feet, falling awkwardly on their backs, heads or hips, like unskilful acrobats, as chance might rule; or engaged themselves in noisy flirtations under the fern-fronds with silent ones of homely hue. Huge flies, ignorant of larders and wire-netting, and quite in a savage state, buzzed about him without knowing that he was a man. In and out of the fern-dells snakes glided in their most brilliant blue and yellow guise, it being the season immediately following the shedding of their old skins, when their colours are brightest. Litters of young rabbits came out from their forms to sun themselves upon hillocks, the hot beams blazing through the delicate tissue of each thin-fleshed ear, and firing it to a blood-red transparency in which the veins could be seen. None of them feared him.

Thomas Hardy
(1840 – 1928)

RETURN OF THE NATIVE

Chapter 6

CHANGE

CHANGE IN THE CHURCH

As churchwarden he was quite an autocrat. For a parson he could respect he would do anything in his power. As an old fashioned churchman, towards such as were responsible for High Church innovations he showed open resentment. One of the most pernicious among the innovators worried him for some time to have the pulpit moved to another site where the preacher might be better seen by the congregation. 'We must do something to get the people to church,' he said. 'Get the people to church!' retorted the warden, 'get the people to church! Time was when they needed no getting. When we had the old fox-hunting parsons here, and the band played, and we sang old fashioned tunes, the fold came of their own accord, and the church was filled. We built a gallery to hold a hundred and twenty more, and that was filled too. The pulpit stood in the middle of the church then, and it did very well. Then a lot of your sort came with new-fangled notions and changed everything. First the pulpit had to be moved towards the chancel; it didn't stand in its right place there, and had to be shifted again. You've taken half the gallery away, and even then you can't half fill the church. Soon there'll be no congregation at all. And all you can suggest is to move the pulpit again. The pulpit will not be moved! It isn't the pulpit, man; the pulpit's all right: it's the damned fools like you who get into it that empty the church.'

J.E. Linnell
(1842 - 1919)

Old Oak

The Vicar

Fiddling and fishing were his arts: at times
He alter'd sermons, and he aim'd at rhymes:
And his fair friends, not yet intent on cards,
Oft he amused with riddles and charades.

    Mild were his doctrines, and not one discourse
But gain'd in softness what it lost in force:
Kind his opinions: he would not receive
An ill report, nor evil act believe;
'If true, 'twas wrong; but blemish great or small
Have all mankind; yea, sinners are we all.'

    If ever fretful thought disturb'd his breast,
If aught of gloom that cheerful mind oppress'd,
It sprang from innovation; it was then
He spake of mischief made by restless men;
Not by new doctrines: never in his life
Would he attend to controversial strife;
For sects he cared not; 'They are not of us,
Nor need we, brethren, their concerns discuss;
But 'tis the change, the schism at home I feel;
Ills few perceive, and none have skill to heal;
Not at the altar our young brethren read
(Facing their flock) the decalogue and creed;
But at their duty, in their desks they stand,
With naked surplice, lacking hood and band:
Churches are now of holy song bereft,
And half our ancient customs changed or left;
Few sprigs of ivy are at Christmas seen,
Nor crimson berry tips the holly's green;
Mistaken choirs refuse the solemn strain
Of ancient Sternhold, which from ours amain
Comes flying forth from aile to aile about,

Sweet links of harmony and long drawn out.'
These were to him essentials; all things anew
He deem'd superfluous, useless, or untrue.

George Crabbe
(1754 – 1832)

from *The Borough*

George Crabbe

CHANGE IN THE COMMUNITY

The schoolmaster was leaving the village, and everybody seemed sorry. The miller at Cresscombe lent him the small white tilted cart and horse to carry his goods to the city of his destination, about twenty miles off, such a vehicle proving of quite sufficient size for the departing teacher's effects. For the schoolhouse had been partly furnished by the managers, and the only cumbersome article possessed by the master, in addition to the packing-case of books, was a cottage piano that he had bought at an auction during the year in which he thought of learning instrumental music. But the enthusiasm having waned he had never acquired any skill in playing, and the purchased article had been a perpetual trouble to him ever since in moving house.

The rector had gone away for the day, being a man who disliked the sight of changes. He did not mean to return till the evening, when the new school-teacher would have arrived and settled in, and everything would be smooth again.

Thomas Hardy
(1840 - 1928)

JUDE THE OBSCURE

In this past decade of social re-orientation the countryside materially has changed more than the town but, paradoxically, it has altered less in spirit. Up to the recent War a touch of feudal system had persisted in the country. The squire and the parson had exercised a leadership derived from their respective offices. Each in his sphere, temporal and spiritual, had wielded the strong influence of benevolent autocrats. That influence is gone. The old squire is dead. His son, perhaps, died too in aeroplane or ship or stricken tank. If he survived physically, he certainly could not continue to survive financially on the concentrated areas of his inheritance. He has moved in most cases to the place of business. The big house is sold to a rootless stranger who had succeeded in that business world, or to an institution, or it had fallen derelict.

If the country folk may no longer look to their squire for practical advice and leadership, neither do they often look to the parson for spiritual guidance. Economic conditions have driven away the squirearchy. Wider education and a broader mental outlook among the parishioners have reduced in their eyes the stature of the parson.

To a great extent the parish has lost its identity now that its problems are not discussed among and solved by the chief figures within its community. Self-government of its own small affairs is nearly lost. The county councils, town-based and urban in their approach, run the rural areas, and in turn they themselves are now run by the metropolitan minds of Westminster and Whitehall, The graded devolution of control from Parliament has now gathered into its fingers more strings than it can adroitly handle. Those far-off parish puppets with a low density of voters to the square mile traditionally un-vocal, suffer the worst inattention.

Thomas Firbank

(b.1910)

Log Hut

Today, there is just one person and she an elderly spinster, who lives in the house where three generations of her forebears lived. There is only one family living in the village whose ancestry in the village goes back four generations. There are six people – I have counted only those who are approaching middle age or who are well past it – living in the houses in which they were born. But when we come to consider the number of village people who were born here and are still living in a different house – still middle-aged or over – we get a mild surprise. They number not less than sixty-four, and I may have missed one or two in counting. That is roughly what the number would have been if a similar count had been made a hundred years ago; hence the surprise. 'Village people contrary to expectation perhaps, have not disappeared. When, however, we consider them as a percentage of people in the village – adding wives and children for this purpose – we find that 'village people' amount to less than 25 per cent of the village population. That, and the fact that one third of my starting total of sixty-four are over seventy years old, amply explains, I think, the increasing take-over of village affairs by the newcomers. The process, I imagine, will go on.

Finally – and here I dare to speak of quality – if we have any doubts about the future, or about the many changes which we have seen in our lives, we have only to look in at the school playground any mid-morning, or see the children as they walk homeward in little groups. These children are healthier, better fed, better clothed, better educated, better behaved, prettier and – did but they know it – happier than any generation of children that ever before walked the village street. For us of the older generation the past is past, and we do not regret it. For them – the future.

Rowland Parker
(1911 – 1989)

The Common Stream

CHANGE ON THE LAND

Cogden farmhouse, rebuilt in the nineteenth century, stands in a dip encircled by gentle slopes. Not only is the land well drained but contains areas of brown earth well suited to wheat and barley growing. In 1813 Robert had good cause to join in the 'general thanksgiving for an immensely productive harvest'. This was the last heartfelt harvest thanksgiving for some time. Although the 1815 Act protected home grown corn, it could not protect the unproductive farmers from the consequences of their inability, whether through lack of capital, intractable soil, mismanagement or misfortune, to meet post-war demands. In this fierce but silent contest carrying on between the productive lands of England and the unproductive, Robert was well equipped to succeed. His business abilities sharpened by a stay in Scotland, enabled him to foresee the possibilities of Cogden which luckily was on the market. Not only was the soil productive and well drained, a great consideration before the factory production of drained pipes, but the fields lay in a block on the Bridport–Weymouth road. Good barley was always in demand as the nineteenth century proved to be the century of ale, while road communication with Weymouth and West Bay made dairy farming and sheep rearing for mutton profitable. Wool, too, was easily marketed at Bridport whence fleeces were sent by carrier to Salisbury and then by canal to London, or, more profitably shipped from West Bay to Poole.

Barbara Kerr

BOUND TO THE SOIL

My grandfather tried farming here; and I gather from his accounts that he sank about £20 per acre in the first three years. That meant draining the ground, and getting it into good condition; and after that he made it pay, except in the years of the potato famine. He writes to my father on 8 March 1846:- 'I should say a diligent clever man, farming his own estate, can make more money now than he could in war time [that is before 1815] for the system of farming is quite changed, and the land is made to produce nearly double what it did then.'

His knowledge of farming was derived from books; and he did things that were not customary here, sometimes with failure, but often with success. Thus, he writes to my father, 2 April 1854:- 'I tilled some barley yesterday... It was another such March fifteen years ago, when I tilled this same field to barley. I then hired horses and gave it a good working; and the weather was so tempting that I tilled it in March to the amusement of my neighbours. The storms in April made it look blue, which amused them still further. But they all acknowledged they could not produce its equal to harvest.'

He writes on 25 April 1843:- 'Folks are waiting to see what spade husbandry will produce. I tell them it's not new to me, for I adopted it elsewhere some twelve or fourteen years ago, and was fully compensated for my trouble. But that will not do: they must see themselves. The field is turned up with the spade, all the spine put under, a foot deep; and I have taken out nearly stones enough to build a wall through the field. The cost in turning is 4d. [per rod] with a quart of cider to a shilling, so with cleaning and bringing it fit for the potato the cost is £4 per acre, about double the old system, which would leave all the stones, and the field not half worked.

'Our farmers are loth to believe that any other method but the old one is beneficial. They fancy all manure is in dung and the like. I tell them the quantity of carbon, etc.,etc... But all will not do: they must see to believe. I have tried 1 cwt. of nitrate of soda on an acre of grass, and it is astonishing the effect it has had.'

On 13 January 1851 he writes:- 'I am trying an experiment, that is, I am fetching every day some of the refuse from the kilns at the Pottery. It is principally burnt clay. I have often looked at it on passing, and fancied it might turn to use – old Cobbett speaks well of burnt clay. My neighbours say they will try it also.'

Cecil Torr
(1857 – 1928)

Small Talk at Wreyland

As I crested the summit of the rise, I came upon old Pooke, a retired farmer well over seventy and a crony of mine for many years. He likes to walk to the brow of the hill every day so that he can see the view, contemplate the fields and take the air into his lungs. He has only had one illness in his life and that was last year. He distils country wisdom; it emanates from him like pine-scent or compressed heather from a tweed coat. He was leaning over a farm-gate gazing at the field in front of him. I passed it on to him that I could not see much to look at. 'Look at it,' said old Pooke, with that animistic sense the countryman has, 'a good-for-nothing.' It was once more a field of rough grazing as it had been in 1938, with this difference that in 1938 it had accumulated a fair store of fertility; now it had none, and that was why it was back in grass. Three successive white crops had finished it. It was part of a farm of 200 acres without a single head of cattle on it, so that the tenant had had plenty of straw but no dung. And it had a sour look, the land, the sulphate of ammonia look, a sort of pinched streaky look, and the grass was nearly all hassocks. Patchy it was too, not a sward, but tussocky. 'Do you know,' said old Pooke, 'in '94 the farmer who had that field used to put forty men on it. Can you see any man about?' (He looked around the wide landscape at our feet.) 'And', he went on, 'I wouldn't put a goat on that field now.' 'Stands to reason,' he concluded after another long and steady look, 'You can't farm land if it's all take and no give.' The old man understood what the professors and economists and technologists have failed to do, that the law of life is give and take, and that the most towering edifice built on the latter principle only, however fortified with reinforced concrete and steel girders, is built on the sand. The problems of production are solved, say the theorists, thinking of their slot-machines.

The age of plenty is with us, all that is needed is a proper machinery of distribution. The earth is conquered; get everybody well-fed, well-housed, well-amused, press that button and out comes Utopia. A pity they can't take a look at that field.

H.J. Massingham
(1888 – 1952)

MEN OF EARTH

Lines written to Martyn Skinner before his Departure from Oxfordshire in Search of Quiet, 1961

Return, return to Ealing,
Worn poet of the farm!
Regain your boyhood feeling
Of uninvaded calm!
For there the leafy avenues
Of limes and chestnut mix'd
Do widely wind, by art designed,
The costly houses 'twixt.

No early morning tractors
The thrush and blackbird drown,
No nuclear reactors
Bulge huge below the down,
No youth upon his motor-bike
His lust for power fulfils,
With dentist's drill intent to kill
The silence of the hills.

In Ealing on a Sunday
Bell-haunted quiet falls,
In Ealing on a Monday
'Milk-o!' the milkman calls;
No lorries grind in bottom gear
Up steep and narrow lanes,
Nor constant here offend the ear
Low-flying aeroplanes.

Return, return to Ealing,
Worn poet of the farm!
Regain your boyhood feeling
Of uninvaded calm!
Where smoothly glides the bicycle
And softly flows the Brent
And a gentle gale from Perivale
Sends up the hayfield scent.

John Betjeman
(1906 – 1984)

DYING OUT

Here you will find the herb-gatherer, most delightful of
cunning rustic men, wise with an ancient wisdom, and possessing
magical secrets. His old, beautiful knowledge is fast dying out.
The country people take patent medicines indiscriminately;
and depend more and more on the quacks. A friend wrote me
the other day of an old man who had been taking Elliman's
Embrocation, but had had to leave off because he found the
price, two-and-sixpence a bottle, too high for him. Yet there
were all about this old man, to be had for the gathering, 'excellent
herbs to heal his pains'. That there should be medicinal values

and virtues in herbs, and plants, and fruits, that the earth should bring forth man's healing as it does his food, is an idea which commends itself to the reason.

R. L. Gales
(1862 - 1927)

VANISHED COUNTRY FOLK

The country potters who were born in the trade have all but vanished, and there are probably less than half a dozen left, though there is a superfluity of artist trained potters making a good living with more sophisticated ware using attractive glazes.

The traditional country potter plied his trade where there was a good supply of suitable clay, whereas the artist-potter first finds his premises and then orders his clay to be delivered by the hundred weight.

A doyen of country potters is Rowland Curtis, in his mid-70's, of Littlethorpe, near Ripon in Yorkshire, who has been at his wheel since leaving school about sixty years ago...

Whereas he used to throw a ton of clay a day, he now works part-time and uses a ton a week, this which his son digs by shovel, is used immediately without any weathering. First the clay is fed into the plugging machine which mixes it up ready for use. A piece of clay is cut off, weighed and then wedged by slamming it down on the bench for a minute or two to eliminate any air bubbles. Mr. Curtis next throws the lump of clay on to his power driven wheel and works it upwards and outwards, so that in five minutes the lump emerges as a smooth and beautifully proportioned pot with a thick lip on top to give it a finish.

As an additional embellishment a coil of clay may be put around the pot and a patterned design added with the fingers, and finally all pots are stamped with the maker's name ...

Mr. Curtis has seen some ups and downs in his time. In the 1920's country potters were kept busy making bread crocks, bowls for setting milk and cooling pots for cream, all of which were glazed. In addition they all made flower pots which can be turned out at an incredible speed. The trade was killed by plastic pots, soil and peat blocks and the potters rapidly went out of business. Mr. Curtis was forced to give up for two years and keep poultry in his pottery sheds, but his one-man business is now thriving. He sells direct, never advertises and cannot cope with the demand, knowing of no competitor within hundreds of miles.

He has occasionally taught his craft in the past, but cannot do so now as he has no diploma. Thus the man with the most experience of throwing pottery in the county is prevented from passing on his skill and knowledge to future generations.

John Manners

The Countryman, Spring 1976

Every village must have two or three men who can turn their hand to most things, including cutting their mates' hair. At one time we had two gentlemen who could perform this service if you went to their homes, while the late Mr. Harsnet, who ran the cycle repair shop, was always ready to oblige with a haircut, but in 1947 George started his own little business. He bought an old bus off his boss, the late Mr L. W. Pudney, which had been used for a meal shed, painted it green and had it stand on the side of the road in Chapel Lane. For many years he did good service, then the rates people came along and George was forced to put up his prices to cover the cost of the rates. He used to charge 6d for men and 3d for children. Our sons, Allan and David, used to love going to see Uncle George for their haircuts every four weeks and there would be a rush to see who could get into the bus first to read the comics, of which George always had a plentiful supply. They never minded how long they had to wait for their turn, which was just as well as it was used very much as a meeting place, especially by the pensioners who were quite happy to sit and discuss the latest news in the village. The business operated every Tuesday and Thursday from 6.00pm till 8.30pm. In the winter months George cut hair by the light of the oil lamps which hung from the roof and the place was kept warm and cosy by the oil stove that stood in one corner. It was a sad day for a great many old village boys when George packed up the business in 1965.

Margaret Cole
(? – 1980)

A COUNTRY GIRL AT HEART

'That's a pack of nonsense,' said the ancient cockle gatherer. 'Our men work on the land, and we women have long before living memory gone down to the sea to get the cockles. I started when I was married, when I wanted extra money to bring up the children; and that's why most of us do it.'

She turned towards the sea and said:

'Those are the last cockle gatherers you'll see in Stiffkey. Girls today want to be ladies. They don't like to get themselves up in such ugly clothes and go down to the sea as their grandmothers did; and they don't like hard work, either... Yes we're the last cockle women, we old ones...'

A look of absolute horror came into the face of this old woman when I asked her if I might take a photograph of her. She put her hands to her eyes as I have seen Arabs do when faced by a camera.

'No, no,' she said, and looked round for cover. I soothed her with great difficulty.

It was not modesty, I think, or the thought of being photographed in such queer garments. Here and there in remote parts of England there exists still a curious belief that to be photographed brings bad luck.

One cockle gatherer came towards me bent beneath the weight of an enormous sack. It was impossible to tell whether this strange figure was that of man or woman. She was wearing a black divided skirt. Thick worsted stockings, wet through with salt water, clung to her legs. She wore a black shawl over her shoulders and a sou'wester that buttoned like a Kate Greenaway bonnet beneath her chin. When I stopped her she lifted her face, and I saw that she was an ancient dame of at least seventy. Her toothless little mouth was pressed primly in below a smooth apple face etched with a million fine lines, and her eyes were blue and childish.

Like many people in this part of England, she was frightened of questions. I asked her if she was strong enough to do such hard work, and she said that she had been doing it since she was a young woman.

A few years ago some one wrote up Stiffkey and its cockle women in a cruel light. It was alleged that intermarriage had so affected the inhabitants that the men did no work while the women slaved to keep things going.

There are few stranger sights in England than the return of these cockle women before the galloping tide. Slowly, heavily, they come with the great dripping sacks of 'Stewkey blues' on their backs. Most are old women, who belong to a tougher generation. Some are middle-aged. Now and again a girl goes down 'for fun', to see how her mother earned extra money to bring her up. The salt spray drenches their short skirts, the wind lashes their bare legs, as they come plodding in over the salt marshes.

H V. Morton
(1892 – 1970)

IN SEARCH OF ENGLAND

Old John The Postman

How well we knew along our road
Old John the postman's sturdy figure,
As on he strode beneath a load
That day by day seemed ever bigger!

How lusty was the note he wound
Afar to herald his appearing!
I often found a sweeter sound
Not so welcome or so cheering.

He was more punctual than the sun,
Whose journeys vary with the seasons,
For John was one who would not shun
His duty for such paltry reasons.

I've seen him white with driven snow;
I've seen him like an otter dripping;
I've known him go when gales would blow
Enough to wreck a fleet of shipping.

Nor did he falter when the heat
Might melt the wax that sealed the letters;
His faithful feet upon their beat
Were aye a lesson to his betters.

For forty years and twelve miles a day;
Compute, you are a calculator;
He trudged away I fear to say
How many times round the Equator.

But John was not the man to range
A yard beyond his wonted tether;
He thought us strange to 'need a change'
He had his changes in the weather.

What lay before his narrow view
He saw with eye not superficial,
And from it due conclusions drew
In language sober and judicial.

He knew the story of the squire;
He knew the troubles of the peasant;
And no grandsire in all the shire,
Had more to tell of past and present.

Ah! not again at eve or morn
Shall he bring me a friend's epistle;
His trusty horn is left forlorn;
The new man blows a penny whistle.

Now John a pensioner of State,
A veteran, though not of battle,
Reclines his weight against a gate,
And meditates upon the cattle.

Yet sometimes when the air is boon,
To taste the fullness of his leisure,
He'll don at noon his posting shoon
And go the ancient round for pleasure.

L'envoy.
So when at last we too lay by
Our letter bags of good intentions,
May you and I, emerite
As honestly have earned our pensions.

R.H. Law

NOTHING OF THE TOWN

MOVING OUT

George Pontifere might have been brought up as a carpenter
and succeeded in no other way than in succeeding his father as
one of the minor magistrates of Paleham, and yet have been a
more truly successful man than he actually was for I take it
there is not much more solid success in the world than what
fell to the lot of old Mr and Mrs Pontifere: it happened, however,
that about the year 1780, when George was a boy of fifteen, a
sister of Mrs Pontifere who had married a Mr Fairlie, came to
pay a few days' visit at Paleham. Mr Fairlie was a publisher,
chiefly of religious works, and had an establishment in

Paternoster Row; he had risen in life and his wife had risen with him...A quick, intelligent boy with a good address, a sound constitution and coming of respectable parents has a potential value which a practised businessman who has need of subordinates is little likely to overlook. Before his visit was over Mr Fairlie proposed to the lad's father and mother that he should put him into his own business, at the same time promising that if the boy did well he should not want someone to bring him forward. Mrs Pontifere had her son's interest too much at heart to refuse such an offer, so the matter was soon arranged, and about a fortnight after the Fairlies had left, George was sent up by coach to London, where he was met by his uncle and aunt, with whom it was arranged that he should live.

This was George's great start in life. He now wore more fashionable clothes than he had yet been accustomed to, and any little rusticity of gait or pronunciation which he had brought from Paleham was so quickly and completely lost that it was ere long impossible to detect that he had not been born and bred among people of what is commonly called education.

Samuel Butler
(1836 – 1902)

THE WAY OF ALL FLESH

We all trooped down to the station, of course; it is only in later years that the farce of 'seeing people off' is seen in its true colours. Edward was the life and soul of the party; and if his gaiety struck one at times as being a trifle over done, it was not a moment to be critical. As we tramped along, I promised him I would ask Farmer Larkin not to kill any more pigs till he came back for the holidays, and he said he would send me a proper catapult – the real article, not a kid's plaything. Then suddenly, when we were about half-way down, one of the girls fell a-snivelling.

The happy few who dare to laugh at the woes of sea-sickness will perhaps remember how, on occasion, the sudden collapses of a fellow-voyager before their very eyes has caused them hastily to revise their self-confidence and resolve to walk more humbly for the future. Even so it was with Edward, who turned his head aside, feigning an interest in the landscape. It was but for a moment; then he recollected the hat he was wearing – a hard bowler, the first of that sort he had ever owned. He took it off, examined it and felt it over. Something about it seemed to give him strength, and he was a man once more.

At the station Edward's first care was to dispose his boxes on the platform so that every one might see the labels and the lettering thereon. One did not go to school for the first time every day! Then he read both sides of his ticket carefully; shifted it to every one of his pockets in turn; and finally fell to chinking of his money, to keep his courage up. We were all dry of conversation by this time, and could only stand round and stare in silence at the victim decked for the altar. And as I looked at Edward, in new clothes of a manly cut, with hard hat upon his head, a railway ticket in one pocket, and money of his own in the other – money to spend as he liked and no questions asked – I began to feel dimly how great was the gulf already yawning betwixt us. Fortunately I was not old enough to realize, further, that here on this little platform the old order lay at its last gasp, and that Edward might come back to us, but it would not be the Edward of yore, nor could things ever be the same again.

When the train steamed up at last, we all boarded it impetuously, with the view of selecting the one peerless carriage to which Edward might be entrusted with the greatest comfort and honour; and as each one found the ideal compartment at the same moment, and vociferously maintained its merits, he stood some chance for a time of being left behind. A porter settled the matter by heaving him through the nearest door; and as the train moved off, Edward's head was thrust out of the window, wearing on it an unmistakable first-quality grin that he had been saving up somewhere for the supreme moment. Very small and white his face looked, on the long side of the retreating train. But the grin was visible, undeniable, stoutly maintained; till a curve swept him from our sight, and he was borne away in the dying rumble, out of our placid backwater, out into the busy world of rubs and knocks and competition, out into the New Life.

Kenneth Grahame
(1859 – 1932)

THE GOLDEN AGE

'Come to Canada with me, Mother,' said Adam roughly. 'Come with me'...

Hannah heard her mother sob, 'I can't, I can't. I hate to lose you, but I've got to stay here. Perhaps if you make your fortune you'll come back to see me one day.'

There was a scrape of chair legs on the floor and I heard her brother saying in a choked voice, 'I'll do well. I'm determined on that. Don't worry, Mother.' Then Hannah slipped off into the garden, not wanting to be found eavesdropping.

He left next day and his mother and sister accompanied him to Melrose station where, with his brass-bound chest neatly labelled for the ship that was to carry him across the Atlantic, he boarded the train for Liverpool. As she looked at her son, Aylie realized that it had always been inevitable she would lose him. He was too good, too ambitious and too intelligent to settle for the life of a labourer, which was all that was open to him at home. Adam had been a good scholar but he left school at twelve to train as a shepherd with a relative of the Cannon family in the Cheviot Hills. He had the makings of a good shepherd but as he stared out over the empty expanse of hills that surrounded him, he felt his life was being wasted. Eventually he saved enough money to pay for a passage to Canada where there were already many Borderers living. From what he heard, it seemed that Canada was a glorious land of opportunity and Adam Kennedy was determined to make good. He was no stranger to hard work and it did not frighten him. His only regret was leaving his mother and sister, but when he spoke about those doubts, Aylie pressed him to go. She saw that it was his only chance.

As he kissed and clung to them on the station platform, Aylie kept outwardly calm though she felt her heart was breaking once again. Her son had always been her most loved child, the one with whom she felt the closest affinity. Now, as he left her, it seemed that her life was one of continual partings.

Elisabeth McNeill
(b.1931)

Lark Returning

It was in this year that Charlie Malcolm, Mrs Malcolm's eldest son, was sent to be a cabin-boy in the Tobacco trader, a three masted ship, that sailed between Port-Glasgow and Virginia in America. She was commanded by Captain Dickie, an Irville man; for at that time the Clyde was supplied with the best sailors from our coast, the coal-trade with Ireland being a better trade for bringing up good mariners than the long voyages in the open sea; which was the reason, as I often heard said, why the Clyde shipping got so many of their men from our country side. The going to sea of Charlie Malcolm was, on divers accounts, a very remarkable thing to us all; for he was the first that ever went from our parish, in the memory of man, to be a sailor, and everybody was concerned at it, and some thought it was a great venture of his mother to let him, his father having been lost at sea. But what could the forlorn widow do? She had five weans, and little to give them; and, as she herself said, he was aye in the hand of his Maker, go where he might; and the will of God would be done, in spite of all earthly wiles and devices to the contrary.

On the Monday morning, when Charlie was to go away to meet the Irville carrier on the road, we were all up, and I walked by myself from the manse into the clachan to bid him farewell, and I met him just coming from his mother's door, as blithe as a bee, in his sailor's dress, with a stick, and a bundle tied in a Barcelona silk handkerchief hanging o'er his shoulder, and his two little brothers were with him, and his sisters, Kate and Effie, looking out from the door all begreeten; but his mother was in the house, praying to the Lord to protect her orphan, as she afterwards told me. All the weans of the clachan were gathered at the kirkyard yett to see him pass, and they gave him three great shouts as he was going by; and everybody was at their doors, and said something encouraging to him; but there was a great laugh when auld Mizy Spaewell came hirpling with her bauchle in her hand, and flung it after him for good-luck.

John Galt
(1779 – 1839)

ANNALS OF THE PARISH

The lads in their hundreds to Ludlow come in for the fair,
There's men from the barn and the forge and the mill and
the fold,
The lads for the girls and the lads for the liquor are there,
And there with the rest are the lads that will never be old.

There's chaps from the town and the field and the till and the
cart.
And many to count are the stalwart, and many the brave,
And many the handsome of face and the handsome of heart,
And few that will carry their looks or their truth to the grave.

I wish one could know them, I wish there were tokens to tell
The fortunate fellows that now you can never discern;
And then one could talk with them friendly and wish them
   farewell
And watch them depart on the way that they will not return.

But now you may stare as you like and there's nothing to scan;
And brushing your elbow unguessed-at and not to be told
They carry back bright to the coiner the mintage of man,
The lads that will die in their glory and never be old.

A.E. Housman
(1859 – 1936)

from A Shropshire Lad
Stanza XVIII

BEING MOVED OUT

It was in a hollow way, near the top of a steep ascent, upon the verge of the Ellangowan estate, that Mr Bertram met the gipsy procession. Four or five men formed the advanced guard, wrapped in long loose great-coats that hid their tall slender figures, as the large slouched hats, drawn over their brows, concealed their wild features, dark eyes, and swarthy faces. Two of them carried long fowling-pieces, one wore a broadsword without a sheath, and all had the highland dirk, though they did not wear that weapon openly or ostentatiously. Behind them followed the train of laden asses, and small carts, or tumblers as they were called in that country, on which were laid the decrepit and the helpless, the aged and infant part of the exiled community. The women in their red cloaks and straw hats, the elder children with bare heads and bare feet, and almost naked bodies, had the immediate care of the little caravan. The road was narrow, running between two broken banks of sand...

When the Laird had pressed on with difficulty among a crowd of familiar faces, which had on all former occasions marked his approach with the reverence due to that of a superior being, but in which he now only read hatred and contempt, and had got clear of the throng, he could not help turning his horse, and looking back to mark the progress of their march...

The van had already reached a small and stunted thicket, which was at the bottom of the hill, and which gradually hid the line of march until the last stragglers disappeared.

His sensations were bitter enough. The race, it is true, which he had thus summarily dismissed from their ancient place of refuge, was idle and vicious; but had he endeavoured to render them otherwise? They were not more irregular characters now, than they had been while they were admitted to consider themselves as a sort of subordinate dependants of his family;

and ought the mere circumstance of his becoming a magistrate to have made at once such a change in his conduct towards them? Some means of reformation ought at least to have been tried, before sending seven families at once upon the wide world, and depriving them of a degree of countenance which withheld them at least from atrocious guilt. There was also a natural yearning of heart on parting with so many known and familiar faces; and to this feeling Godfrey Bertram was peculiarly accessible, from the limited qualities of his mind, which sought its principal amusements among the petty objects around him. As he was about to turn his horse's head to pursue his journey, Meg Merrilies, who had lagged behind the troop, unexpectedly presented herself.

She was standing upon one of those high precipitous banks, which, as we before noticed, overhung the road; so that she was placed considerably higher than Ellangowan, even though he was on horseback; and her tall figure, relieved against the clear blue sky, seemed almost of supernatural stature. We have noticed that there was in her general attire, or rather in her mode of adjusting it, somewhat of a foreign costume, artfully adopted perhaps for the purpose of adding to the effect of her spells and predictions, or perhaps from some traditional notions respecting the dress of her ancestors. On this occasion, she had a large piece of red cotton cloth rolled about her head in the form of a turban, from beneath which her dark eyes flashed with uncommon lustre. Her long and tangled black hair fell in elf-locks from the folds of this singular head-gear. Her attitude was that of a sibyl in frenzy, and she stretched out in her right hand a sapling bough, which seemed just pulled.

'I'd be d—d,' said the groom, 'if she has not been cutting the young ashes in the Dukit park!' – The Laird made no answer, but continued to look at the figure which was thus perched above his path.

'Ride your ways,' said the gipsy, 'ride your ways, Laird of Ellangowan – ride your ways, Godfrey Bertram! – This day have ye quenched seven smoking hearths – see if the fire in your ain parlour burn the blither for that. Ye have riven the thack off seven cottar houses – look if your ain roof-tree stand the faster. – Ye may stable your stirks in the shealings at Derncleugh – see that the hare does not couch on the hearthstane at Ellangowan. – Ride your ways, Godfrey Bertram what do ye glower after our fold for? – There's thirty hearts there, that wad hae wanted bread ere ye had wanted sunkets, and spent their life-blood ere ye had scratched your finger.

'Yes – there's thirty yonder, from the auld wife of an hundred to the babe that was born last week, that ye have turned out o' their bits o' bields, to sleep with the tod and the blackcock in the muirs! – Ride your ways, Ellangowan. – Our bairns are hinging at our weary backs – look that your braw cradle at hame be the fairer spread up: not that I'm wishing ill to little Harry, or to the babe that's yet to be born – God forbid – and make them kind to the poor, and better folk than their father! – And now, ride e'en your ways; for these are the last words ye'll ever hear Meg Merrilies speak, and this is the last reise that I'll ever cut in the bonny woods of Ellangowan.'

So saying, she broke the sapling she held in her hand, and flung it into the road. Margaret of Anjou bestowing on her triumphant foes her keen-edged malediction, could not have turned from them with a gesture more proudly contemptuous. The laird was clearing his voice to speak, and thrusting his hand in his pocket to find a half-crown; the gipsy waited neither for his reply nor his donation, but strode down the hill to overtake the caravan.

Ellangowan rode pensively home; and it was remarkable that he did not mention this interview to any of his family. The groom was not so reserved; he told the story at great length to a full audience in the kitchen, and concluded by swearing, that 'if ever the devil spoke by the mouth of a woman, he had spoken by that of Meg Merrilies that blessed day'.

Sir Walter Scott
(1771 - 1832)

Guy Mannering

Dolly survived, but utterly broken, hollow-chested, a workhouse fixture. Still, so long as she could stand she had to wash in the laundry; weak as she was, they weakened her still further with steam and heat, and labour. Washing is hard work for those who enjoy health and vigour. To a girl, broken in heart and body, it is a slow destroyer. Heat relaxes all the fibres; Dolly's required bracing. Steam will soften wood and enable the artificer to bend it to any shape. Dolly's chest became yet more hollow; her cheek bones prominent; she bent to the steam. This was the girl who had lingered in the lane to help the boy pick watercress, to gather a flower, to listen to a thrush, to bask in the sunshine. Open air and green fields were to her life itself. Heart miseries are always better borne in the open air. How just, how truly scientific, to shut her in a steaming wash-house!

The workhouse was situated in a lovely spot, on the lowest slope of hills, hills covered afar with woods. Meads at hand, corn-fields farther away, then green slopes over which broad cloud-shadows glided slowly. The larks sang in spring, in summer the wheat was golden, in autumn the distant woods were brown and red and yellow. Had you spent your youth in those fields, had your little drama of life been enacted in them, do you not think that you would like at least to gaze out at them from the windows of your prison? It was observed that the miserable wretches were always looking out of the windows in this direction. The windows on that side were accordingly built up and bricked in that they might not look out.

Richard Jefferies
(1848 – 1887)

LIFE OF THE FIELDS

The old blue-painted caravan squatting by the side of the lane, and always something for sale in the table by the gate. In winter, sprays of red-berried holly stuck in an enamelled jug, '5p a spray', the cardboard notice held in place by half a brick. Early spring and pussy willow took pride of place with primroses bunched at 10p. As the seasons changed, so Annie's table reflected the changes. Little punnets of home-grown strawberries and raspberries, a few pinks in a jam jar, the first blackberries, elderberries and even sloes.

Annie lived quite alone in the small caravan. Almost hidden by the hedge the plume of smoke from the chimney swept across the ploughed field. The gulls cried and wheeled overhead. A lonely place. Inside the caravan was spotless, if a little crowded with the collection of a lifetime. Ornaments, books and piles of magazines and papers filled any available space. The old comfy chair, cushioned at the back and sides to keep out the draughts, was pulled up in front of the black stove, its long chimney poking through the roof. Annies's bunk bed was covered by a patchwork quilt, not of her making. Annie was not the patchwork type. On the narrow window sill, a jar of wild flowers: buttercups, ox-eye daisies, meadowsweet. Annie loved the countryside: not for her the fancy arrangements.

Any day, winter or summer, she could be seen pedalling along the lanes on her ancient sit-up-and-beg bicycle.

I suppose the village people called her Berry Annie because she made a little extra money gathering blackberries, elderberries and during the war, rose hips. As they were then a valuable source of vitamin C, a grateful government paid a few shillings to anyone who would pick them. It was very rough, prickly work, but Annie did it.

She wore her faded black hat pulled well down over her ears, wisps of grey hair forever escaping from the confines of a bun. In her man's long fawn mac and knitted mittens, she was a familiar figure and on her arms there was always a basket. Annie combed the hedges and pieces of common-land for the choicest blackberries and sold them to the roadside stalls, which, until a couple of years ago, flourished in this part of the country. Any surplus was put out for sale on the table.

Annie was always ready for a chat, and spoke in a cultured voice that belied her appearance and came as quite a shock to strangers. She had travelled in her life, living for some time in America. In all the years I knew her she dressed exactly the same. Being a faithful customer at the village jumble sales, I suppose she bought another black hat and man's mac when the old ones wore out. Social Security she had either never heard of or ignored. Her needs were simple. She gathered the necessary firewood from the fields and woods and grew a few vegetables in the patch by the caravan. Money was only needed for essentials such as bread and milk, and a little meat for a stew.

I suddenly realised that I hadn't seen her for some time, and come to think of it, the caravan had gone too.

'What happened to her?' I asked. 'Didn't you know? They moved her to a council flat.'

Jeannie Pomeroy
The Countryman,
Winter 1981–2

INTO THE COUNTRY

Nothing had prepared him for the sight of the small stone house, and the yard with the bits of broken machinery in it. At the door stood his grandfather, old and stooped, and wearing shabby old clothes, a torn jacket and no collar on his shirt. Beside him was Uncle Vincent, a taller and younger version but wearing a suit that looked as if it were respectable.

'You're welcome to your own place,' Grandpa Doyle had said. 'This is the land you children came from, it's a grand thing to have you back from all those red buses and crowds of people to walk your own soil again.'

Grandpa Doyle had been to London once on a visit. Brendan knew that because of the pictures, the one on the wall taken outside Buckingham Palace, and the many in the albums. He couldn't really remember the visit. Now as he looked at these two men standing in front of the house he felt an odd sense of having come home. Like those children's stories he used to read when an adventure was coming to an end and they were coming out of the forest. He was afraid to speak in case it would ruin it.

They stayed a week there that time. Grandpa Doyle had been frail, and hadn't walked very much further than his front door. But Vincent had taken them all over the place. Sometimes in the old car with its bockety trailer; the trailer had not changed since that first visit. Sometimes Vincent couldn't be bothered to untackle it from the car even though there might be no need to transport a sheep, and it rattled along comfortingly behind them.

Even way back then, Brendan had noticed that Vincent had never bothered to explain to people who they were; he didn't fuss and introduce them as his brother's children, explain that they were over here for a week's visit, that in real life they lived in a lovely leafy suburb of North London called Pinner, and that they played tennis at the weekends in the summer. Mother and Father would have managed to tell all that to almost anyone. Vincent just went on the way he always did, talking little, replying slowly and effortlessly when he was asked a question.

Brendan got the feeling that he'd prefer not to be asked too many questions. Sometimes, even on that holiday, he and Vincent had walked miles together with hardly a word exchanged. It was extraordinarily restful.

He hated it when the week was over.

'Maybe we'll come back again,' he had said to Vincent as they left.

'Maybe.' Vincent hadn't sounded sure.

'Why do you think we might not?' They were leaning on a gate to the small vegetable area. There were a few drills of potatoes there and easy things like cabbage and carrots and parsnips. Things that wouldn't kill you looking after them, Vincent had explained.

'Ah, there was a lot of talk about you all coming back here, but I think it came to nothing. Not after they saw the place.'

Brendan's heart skipped.

'Coming back ... for more than a holiday do you mean?'

'Wasn't that what it was all about?'

'Was it?'

He had seen his uncle's eyes looking at him kindly.

'Yerra, don't worry yourself, Brendan boy, just live your life the best you can, and then one day you can go off and be where people won't be getting at you.'

'When would that day be?'

'You'll know when it arrives,' Vincent had said without taking his eyes away from the few rows of potatoes.

And indeed Brendan had known when that day arrived.

Maeve Binchy
(b.1940)

SILVER WEDDING

He was celebrating Plough Monday by steering a straight furrow. His uniform consisted of tweed jacket and cap, and gumboots over jodhpurs. When strangers are informed that he is seventy years old they refuse to believe it, at any rate until they have approached near enough to notice the tracery of lines at the corner of his eyes. Then they exclaim: 'He's either a farmer or a sailor.' In fact, he is both, having been invalided after wounds received when his destroyer engaged an Italian cruiser.

Like many other mariners, the Commander beached himself within sight of the sea that was his calling and is still his recreation. There he works a fifty-hour week, farming a small property as he commanded his ship, which is to say rigorously, justly, and with a flair that transcends mere efficiency. Some farms in the district are unkempt, but on the Commander's land everything is shipshape. You never see a plough capsized midfield nor a sheet of tin plugging a broken hedge. Other farmers fasten their gates with twine, but the Commander's gates are painted white, and the latch is greased.

No industrial disputes trouble the farm, chiefly because the two part-time hands are industrious, being respectively an ex-Marine, aged sixty-five, and the Commander's former steward, aged sixty-six (known as 'Hobbly' because he lost a leg at Dunkirk). To watch the three veterans working alongside is to perceive the brotherhood of man and the difference between men. They indulge neither familiarity nor contempt, but follow the rule of the sea whereby one commands, and all obey. If neighbouring farmers complain that their own men are lazy or negligent, the Commander smiles, and says nothing. When he does speak, it is briefly, dryly, conclusively.

J.H. B. Peel
(1913 – 1983)

NEW COUNTRY TALK

'Sell it, make a profit and start having some fun, dear!'

'You could let it as a holiday cottage, rent the land out for grazing and make a tidy little living, you know.'

'For God's sake just get rid of it!'

The–well-meant advice from friends came blowing cool sense into my fevered brain, and before I actually got back to it, to sell the farm had been my firm intention. Despite all the hard, slogging work I'd put in, there was as much debt as ever hanging over me, and the thought of the £25,000 the place was now valued at seemed a glorious and instant solution to all my problems.

I'd forgotten, though, the heart-gripping splendour of that wonderful composition of mountain and hill and field and wood and river. When I saw it again after so long away, I realised that to talk about selling was one thing – doing it was going to be quite another matter. Apart from which, the sight of those forlorn animals made the idea of sending them on to yet another uncertain future unbearable. Which was all very well, but how was I going to keep them? I certainly had no money to employ anyone and, with my work prospects at an all-time low, I wouldn't even be able to keep myself unless I was on hand in London to take any jobs offered.

'You'll give yourself a nervous breakdown if you don't quit going round in circles,' said Sue, who'd relieved her feelings during the past twenty-four hours by chopping up a great mound of wood and sorting out the rocks for a stone wall. 'Well, me and my van are off to Holland and all points east. I wonder what you'll be doing in the next few months.' And that was the last we ever saw of her except that Mrs P. who happened to be collecting Green Shield stamps, got a couple of envelopes of them from odd parts of the country.

During all my distracted meanderings around the farm, Meta and Alan Bonney had said very little, although I'd noticed them whispering quietly to each other. Now they came up with a remarkable offer. If I could leave them the use of my old car while I was back in London and Mrs P. stayed to keep her company, Meta would live at the farm and get it back on its feet while Alan coped alone with their goat farm. They wanted no payment, just the assurance that I would do everything I could to keep the place and its animals intact.

'Give yourself till spring', they urged. 'You never know what might happen then. But you can't just give up. You'll never find another place like this.'

'I know that,' I said wearily, 'but you can't live on a view. Even Cliff Griffiths, who had the rest of the land and is an experienced farmer, had to take another job to make any kind of living here. I don't mind doing that but the humiliating fact is, I'm totally unemployable outside of broadcasting.'

Meta, who has to be one of life's great optimists, then put into words something that had been lurking dangerously at the back of my mind. 'What about that country programme you've been so keen about?' she asked. 'Let's face it, at the moment you don't really know much about the day-to-day problems of running a small place. If you were to get down to it, those people at the BBC might take a bit more notice of you. The Bank Holiday programmes are all very pleasant, but they're very much a townsperson's view of what living on a farm is all about, aren't they?'

God help me, it was the very excuse I was looking for! If I'd known then how much longer it was going to take to convince 'those people at the BBC', I'd have followed Sue and her van out of the gate and never come back.

Jeanine McMullen

My Small Country Living

I do not know how it came about, but at school one day we were asked if any of us would like to go to the country for a fortnight. The cost would be 2s. 1d. each. If we wanted to go we could pay into the penny bank which was held at school. You could pay a penny or more, as you could afford it. My parents consented to my sister and I going and each week on Monday morning in went our precious pennies, until we had enough to pay for both of us to go. My mother patched and altered and sewed until she was satisfied we had enough clothes to last us the fortnight. I think about twelve children went in all. We travelled by train to a place called Childrey. I do not remember what county it was in, but I recall it as a small village consisting of only a few cottages. On arrival at the small country station we were met by a group of country women, who looked us over and then chose which child she would take. I refused to go with any of them unless Kathleen came too. I had been told to look after her as she was younger than I. Now each woman had expected to take only one child and had room for no more. There we stood, refusing to be separated, until a kindly woman came and said she would have us if we did not mind being crowded a bit.

Great was our relief to know that somebody wanted us. She took us home to her small cottage. There was the kitchen in which we all lived, and two bedrooms upstairs, one for her and her husband and one for the children. She had three girls of about our age with whom we shared a large double bed. This was contrived by putting the two of us at the wrong end of the bed. We had great fun sleeping five in one bed. On the first night we were greatly surprised to see them undress and get into bed with no nightdresses. They in turn were most amused to see us put ours on. They asked us what they were, for they had never worn such things and always stripped all their clothes off before tumbling into bed. Nightdresses were unheard of in that family.

Grace Foakes
(b.1901)

BETWEEN HIGH WALLS

As the weeks passed and the sun continued to beat on the baking façade of the great house, there were many things he discovered about himself and not the least important of them was the durability of the bright crystals of thought left in the recesses of his brain by the long, exhausting fever duel between the static army on the ceiling and the serenity of the view of the park and downland, seen through the windows of the two wards he had occupied. Somehow the latter came to represent his future, and all that was pleasant and rewarding in life, and he saw it not simply as a pleasing vista of fields, woods and browsing cattle, but as a vision of England he had remembered and yearned for out there on the scorching veldt. And this, in itself, was strange, for he was city born and bred, and although he had never shared the Cockney's pride in the capital neither had he been conscious, as a boy, of a closer affinity with the woods and hedgerows of the farmland on the Kent-Surrey border, where he had spent his childhood and boyhood. Yet the pull existed now, and it was a very strong pull, as though he owed his life to nectar sucked from the flowers growing wild out there across the dreaming fields near the rim of the woods, and with this half-certainty came another – that it was in a setting like this that he must let the years rescued for him unwind, yielding some kind of fulfilment or purpose. He had never had thoughts like this before and it occurred to him that pain, and a prolonged flirtation with death, had matured him in a way that had been leap-frogged by the other convalescents, many of whom had had more shattering experiences in the field. Some the war had left cynical and a few, among them the permanently maimed, bitter, but all the regular officers seemed to have emerged from the war with their prejudices intact and talked of little else but sport, women, and the military lessons learned from the campaigns. They continued, Paul thought, to regard England as a jumping-off ground for an eternal summer holiday in the sun among lesser breeds, looking to them and the Empire for protection and economic stability, but had little or no sense of kinship with the sun-drenched fields beyond the terrace, or the chawbacons seen toiling there, taking advantage of the Coronation weather to cut and stack the long grass.

R.F. Delderfield
(1912 - 1972)

A Horseman Riding By

From the coffee-and-biscuits at eight-thirty to the tea-and home-made-madeira-cake at ten, the evening went off swimmingly. Ralph Wetherall turned out to be a trim plump man of about forty with gleaming iron-grey hair and a softly-tended ruddy complexion. He seemed anxious to learn all the other men could tell him about village personalities and affairs, and while not crudely pushing himself forward showed that he would be ready gradually to take in such matters the proper part of the owner of Green Lawns. Meanwhile the three ladies chatted together, Margaret listening interestedly on the outskirts of the group, appreciating though seldom profiting by the kindly efforts Mrs. Wetherall made to drag her into the conversation.

'What made you decide to come and settle in Priory Dean?' asked George Bruce over the teacups, when the conversation conventionally became general between the sexes.

'Pure chance,' Mr Wetherall replied. 'We wanted to be some little way out of London for the sake of the children, but not so far that I couldn't get in every day. We'd started looking south of the river and couldn't find anything that took our fancy, and then one day I ran into a man at the club – but you must know him, young Alan Thatcher of Thatchers and Son?'

'I've met him once or twice,' said Gerald a little uneasily. The Thatchers of Bentworth Park with their Rolls-Royce and their herd of pedigree Jerseys were simultaneously admired for their wealth and position, despised for being of the new urban aristocracy who kept themselves to themselves and played no part in the life of the countryside.

Mr Wetherall went on, 'Well, it was he who suggested we should try Priory Dean. "It's one of the few unspoilt villages within twenty miles of London," he said to me, and by Jove he was right. Martha and I fell in love with it as soon as we saw it.

Those houses round the village green now, they're real gems. Martha fell for that big Georgian one in the middle – the doctor's house, isn't it? – but I said to her, better to have some modern conveniences and keep the others for looking at.' He laughed heartily and the ladies fell to praising Green Lawns, its admirable modernity, the ease with which it could be run.

'But we don't know how much longer the village will stay unspoilt,' said George Bruce with a sigh. 'They've only put up those ugly shops along the Arcade in the past twenty years, and now we hear there's some talk of a new housing estate along Archery Lane. I'm afraid the character of the village is changing, there's no doubt about that.'

'I don't know that there's any harm in it,' said Ralph Wetherall, 'so long as they don't over-build. There seems to be no doubt that the overflow from London's got to go somewhere, and all these people should bring some money into the village.'

'We've always rather prided ourselves on not just being a London dormitory,' said Gerald with dignity. 'Most of the people living here work locally, and we've rather felt it will destroy the character of the place if we get a lot of people whose interests lie outside.'

Marghanita Laski
(1915 – 1988)

THE VILLAGE

Two newcomers to the business of running a village shop were among the winners in Staffordshire's National Girobank Village Shop Competition.

First prize for the Brightest Food Shop and General Store went to the youngest competitor in the contest. He's 19 year old Adrian Williams, who runs the village stores in Brindley

Ford, and had only been trading for ten months. He also received an award as runner-up in the Best Shop Under New Management section.

Adrian had three jobs after leaving school and decided, after being unemployed for twelve months, to set up on his own. With some financial help from his parents and his own small savings, he took over the store in Brindley Ford. 'It was a bit of a risk' he says, 'but it's paid off'. It means working, as every village shopkeeper knows, long hours seven days a week but 'it's definitely worth it', he says.

Neither Adrian nor Derek Leeming, of Leemings Store and Post Office in Tittensor, had had any experience of the grocery trade before they began their business. Derek, who won first prize for the best new service to customers, moved from Liverpool just over a year ago after being in the printing trade. He provides a delivery service, and a prescription collection service for customers.

'We try to provide what people need', he says. 'We're in the business to survive and make a living, so we have to find ways of attracting customers from the large supermarkets. We've built up the delicatessen side of the store with home cooked meats and fresh vegetables, and people come into the shop just to buy those items and purchase a few more things whilst they are there.'

Derek believes that having a sense of humour is important. 'I like to make people feel a little better and more cheerful for having come into the store,' he says. And there's no doubt that Derek's recipe for success is a good one. He paid tribute to all his customers in Tittensor. 'They're marvellous people – they've given me so much support in my first year, and I wouldn't swop them for all the tea in China.'

Melting Pot No. 13, Autumn 1984
<u>Staffordshire Community Council Magazine</u>

Chapter 7

SPIRIT

HOSPITALITY AND KINDNESS

If the postman, the rector, the girl groom, the gamekeeper's daughter and the schoolmaster's brother are gathered together to drink coffee with the lady of the house and discuss the Common Market, the choice of carnival queen, the incidence of smoker's cough, or anything else, several propositions may be taken for granted.

They are likely to be in our kitchen. If they are not, they will be in somebody else's kitchen. And if they are indeed in somebody else's kitchen, then others forming a similarly mixed company will be in our kitchen, socializing. For that, as much as preparation of food, is what country kitchens are for. He is an imprudent man who imagines, as I did, that he can nip in with his breakfast tray, leave it, and go about his business. If he has any such ambition he should pause outside the door, and if he hears a burble of voices, retreat pussyfoot. Otherwise he will shortly find himself burbling too, and to disengage from burbling is no light matter.

Having naïvely walked in and found the company assembled as stated, thus becoming trapped, it was interesting to disentangle the ostensible from the true reasons for the presence of each coffee drinker. Experience has made me a realist. So discrepancies were to be expected. They were illuminating.

The rector, a poor liar by clerical standards, had just dropped in because he had not run across us lately. A likely tale. In fact, he had seen that the lady of the house was next on the roster for church flowers, and wished to discover if the operation had yet reached the planning stage. She has never actually failed in her duty, but she is apt to leave her effort as late as Harry Wragg the jockey used to do. The girl groom is there because she has a nose like a pointer. She can wind a brew of coffee at 60 yards, and did. So she came to ask whether the saddle cloths are out of the Bendix yet. If they had not been, there would have been time to put them in, switch on, rinse them, dry them and iron them before she stops speaking for the rising generation.

The postman is there because he had a package too large for the letter box, so had to ring. He would have been there even if he had not had to ring. All suspect that without this routine fortification of his energies, he would flake out before the next house. The gamekeeper's daughter has arrived for professional reasons. She stumps the country setting, perming, and in other ways refurbishing the crowning glory of every belle for miles. Be there a dance or a dinner party her book must be made up far in advance, and subtle are the stratagems employed to secure the latest possible appointment.

The schoolmaster's brother specializes in discovering urgent jobs on other people's property. As, for instance, the blocked ditch about which I had done nothing, well knowing that in the fullness of time he would. So he came in the guise of a supplicant wondering whether I could spare a few Christmas Drumheads as a lead-in to a discussion on recompense.

Whatever their purpose none could have been present had they not possessed qualifying status. To define this is impossible. Kitchen coffee coteries are not composed on the principle of too grand or not grand enough. We have had the Lord Lieutenant in ours, not because he is the Queen's representative, but because he is on the network. The doctor's wife will not gain admittance in a thousand years. The police superintendent will be jovially received, but only in the study. A great cohort of leading ladies are drawing room material, and nothing more.

Yet there are the self-elected many who confidently enter that great crucible of human quality, the kitchen. There they open their hearts, and indeed their mouths, debate issues great and small, and ensure that fingers are kept on the pulse of public affairs, and private ones too, for miles around. Happily we are on other networks, also. To be received by friends at their front door, except on a formal occasion, would be chilling. We go as of right to the kitchen. And we are not alone.

'Proteus'

THE CHANGING YEAR

Just then Mr Holbrook appeared at the door, rubbing his hands in very effervescence of hospitality. He looked more like my idea of Don Quixote than ever, and yet the likeness was only external. His respectable housekeeper stood modestly at the door to bid us welcome; and, while she led the elder ladies upstairs to a bedroom, I begged to look about the garden. My request evidently pleased the old gentleman, who took me all round the place and showed me his six-and-twenty cows, named after the different letters of the alphabet. As we went along, he surprised me occasionally by repeating apt and beautiful quotations from the poets, ranging easily from Shakespeare and George Herbert to those of our own day. He did this as naturally as if he were thinking aloud, and their true and beautiful words were the best expression he could find for what he was thinking or feeling. To be sure he called Byron 'my Lord Byron,' and pronounced the name of Goethe strictly in accordance with the English sound of the letters— "As Goethe says, 'Ye ever-verdant palaces',", &c. Altogether, I never met with a man, before or since, who had spent so long a life in a secluded and not impressive country, with ever-increasing delight in the daily and yearly change of season and beauty.

When he and I went in, we found that dinner was nearly ready in the kitchen – for so I suppose the room ought to be called, as there were oak dressers and cupboards all round, all over by the side of the fireplace, and only a small Turkey carpet in the middle of the flag-floor. The room might have been easily made into a handsome dark oak dining-parlour by removing the oven and a few other appurtenances of a kitchen, which were evidently never used, the real cooking-place being at some distance. The room in which we were expected to sit was a stiffly-furnished, ugly apartment; but that in which we did sit was what Mr Holbrook called the counting-house, where he paid his labourers their weekly wages at a great desk near the door. The rest of the pretty sitting-room – looking into the orchard, and all covered over with dancing tree-shadows – was filled with books. They lay on the ground, they covered the walls, they strewed the table. He was evidently half ashamed and half proud of his extravagance in this respect. They were of all kinds – poetry and wild weird tales prevailing. He evidently chose his books in accordance with his own tastes, not because such and such were classical or established favourites.

'Ah!' he said, 'we farmers ought not to have much time for reading; yet somehow one can't help it.'

Elizabeth Gaskell
(1810 – 1865)

CRANFORD

Good-bye, Mr Farrelly, good-bye indeed. And when we see you next year, I hope you'll be strong again. Strong and well.'

'Yes, indeed, Mr Farrelly.' The deep voice of the farmer joined the chant, as he came across from washing his hands at the tap. 'You want to take care of yourself, and get stout again. Look at the way your coat is hanging. Let us see you filling it out, when you come to us next year.'

'Yes.' Ignatius glanced down himself. 'I have shrunk a bit, haven't I?'

'You have indeed. Your sisters will have to be taking in your suits for you.'

'Oh, but – ' Mrs McRae was afraid Ignatius would be depressed 'It's not much. Mr Farrelly will soon be putting that on again. Once one is well, it's an easy thing to be putting on the weight again.'

'Surely, surely.' The farmer took Ignatius's hand in both of his. 'Come to us, Mr Farrelly, as soon as you are well. We will feed you up. Good scones and butter, plenty of milk, fresh air.'

'Good porridge.'

'Yes.' With an inclination of his head he accepted his wife's addition. 'Good porridge, too. Those are the things that will make you sound and heavy again.'

'Indeed, I'm looking forward to it already.'

Ignatius turned, and looked round the familiar yard. The farm was built in a rectangle, both as a precaution against weather, and to save space. The dwelling house was at the North end. Stables and byres ran down the sides, with rooms for a cowman and a shepherd. Calves, hens, and the farmer's children ran about in the snug enclosure of the yard. A sheepdog sat yawning in the sun. Ignatius remembered that last year too the farmer had come to say good-bye, washing his hands. He had been killing a sheep. The children stood around, absorbedly watching the blood and the last twitchings of the beast as it lay on its back on the table. They were too much absorbed to come and say good-bye. The dogs had been there too, eager, uneasy. Here was the yard, all the same, with the mountain green and towering above it.

'Well. Good-bye, Mr McRae. Good-bye, Mrs McRae. I hate having to go early like this. But then, I hate it whenever I have to go.'

'Indeed, you are very faithful to the place, Mr Farrelly.'

They said no more, but the way they squeezed his hand and the kindness in their eyes spoke their sympathy for his altered state. He walked away from them across the grass, knowing that they were looking after him, knowing how they would shake their heads and exchange a commiserating glance with one another. When he reached the road, he ventured to look back and wave at them. They were standing there, outside the low, whitewashed front of the farm, looking after him.

L.A.G. Strong
(1896 – 1958)

CORPORAL TUNE

And that brings me to the kindliness of Heathley – or should I say rural England? – in my boyhood and youth. For that boyhood I have rarely a nostalgia or regret, it has irretrievably gone and there is little in it that even day-dreams would wish to alter. Nor is there a nostalgia for the scenes of my youth, even those that also are gone, for I have only to close my eyes to summon and behold them. But where there is always for me a poignancy and a regret is in the remembering of people.

Let me make myself perfectly clear. Heathley was no Arcadia. It had its drunkards and it abounded in what I might call promiscuous love, and of such, according to some ancient poets, was the land of Arcadia. But Heathley had also its hypocrites and petty-minded, its sharpers and fawners, its liars and its petty thieves. I say petty because I never remember a burglary in the parish or a theft sufficiently serious to be anything of a wonder, and it is true that most doors in the village were never locked. I remember too, as a small boy, the sensation that was caused when a certain Dick Carter of Stow – a village beyond Brackford – was at large and committing robberies in our countryside. To us children it was as if a werewolf were abroad, and I remember the relief when Carter was finally apprehended, and by – of all people – our own Potter.

But what I do claim is that never have I known a village so full of kindly people, and I make no differentiation between Church or Methodists. Among the Methodists one could discern a kind of communal philanthropy like that that actuated the Quakers; the feeling, so to speak, that Methodist blood was thicker than Church water. And there for me, whether of Church or Chapel, is the poignancy and the regret: that never by any conceivable chance shall I see those people again. To see them with the eye of the mind is of no value, for what I wish is to shake them by the hand, and speak with them, and thank them for what they were and for the kindnesses bestowed with no thought or possibility of reward or even an awareness that they were kindnesses at all.

I remember overhearing the conversation of many a village man in the spring.

'How're you off for plants, George?'

'Not so bad. Might do with a few more savoys, though.'

'Come you along down to mine to-night and you can have some. I got plenty.'

For those plants a village man would have been ashamed to charge his neighbour. And it was the same with seed potatoes. My father, always far too busy with this and that to do the things that really mattered, would inevitably be short of seed potatoes in the spring, but at the last moment he would always remember some neighbour and come back with a pailful.

Michael Home
(b.1885)

<small>SPRING SOWING</small>

There has been much comment from certain quarters about the lack of community spirit. This is just not so. Longnor has and is taking part in community activities. Twice when a reservoir was proposed for building in the Manifold Valley, the scheme was defeated; the bus service still functions due to community pressure, and Parwich Hospital is to be opened again, thanks to the activities of local people in the Moorland Area. There are also eight thriving darts teams in the village run from the Horseshoe, the Crewe and Harpur Arms and the Grapes, which have been very successful in area contests. There is the Thursday Club for the over-sixties, the Brownies with an enthusiastic following, and the under-fives group. There is also an active branch of the British Legion and a recently formed Youth Activity Group. So the community spirit has never died, it has just taken on different forms. One of the greatest characteristics of Longnor and the Moorland area is the friendliness, kindliness and compassion of its people. No one who is sick or in trouble is left to carry their burden alone, there are always people who rally round to help, a communal responsibility.

'Village Voice'
Peak Park News, Spring 1983

TOLERANCE AND GENTLENESS

Tommy's roughness was balanced by his tenderness for birds and animals, and I have seen his eyes soften in wonderment at the sight of a young robin being fed by its parents. Once I saw him half-way up a tall elm, climbing with one hand while the other held a tiny object. 'A baby owl,' he shouted down at me, 'I won't be a minute before I put it back in its nest. You look at the bottom and you'll see two mice its mother must have brought it during the night.' There was the incident of the fox cubs who chose one of our potato meadows as a playground, gambolling at night among the green plants and crushing flat the leaves and stalks. It was the custom in the neighbourhood when this sort of thing happened for the farmer to set traps; and I have seen of an early May morning four cubs each in a corner  of a meadow with a leg caught in a gin. I remember how curious it seemed to me that they did not appear frightened, as if it were still part of the game they had started to play in the night; and they waited there as the sun rose until the farmer, in his own good time, arrived to knock them one by one on the

HENRY
CROW.

head. We, however, were prepared to leave the playground as it was, losing the potatoes to the cubs, but Tommy, on the other hand, was more practical. 'We can't afford to lose the taties,' said he, 'and we mustn't hurt the cubs. I know a way of persuading the vixen to move them to another earth. You leave it to me.' He never told us what he did though I can guess. In any case the meadow was never used as a playground again.

Derek Tangye
(b.1912)

GULL ON THE ROOF

Mr Ponsonby helped us to make the cottage habitable, as he helps us with everything in our lives.

I hope you will like Mr Ponsonby, because he is so shy that you must like him first and get to know him afterwards. There are people like that.

He is big and gentle and clumsy until you set him on to do things, then he isn't clumsy at all, but exceedingly clever and expert with his hands. He is an artist, but never sells his pictures because he is much too shy to ask anybody to buy them. He would think he was asking a favour. Sometimes he gets up courage to give a picture, and by some divine alchemy of modesty he actually makes you feel that you are doing him a great favour by taking it. Yet his pictures are rare, and almost plangent with beauty.

They are all small – strange that such a big man should make those exquisite small paintings – and all of shy, wild things. The plover finding the place to make her nest, the moorhen parting the reeds, the vole eating crowfoot beside the rainy river, the harvest mouse peering with bright eyes round an ear of corn…

And you know how little country boys will stand and frown and look sullenly at you, and then run behind their mother's skirts or their father's back and from that vantage-point suddenly smile at you a wide, sweet smile? He has a lovely picture of just such a little boy – sun-tanned skin, sun-bleached hair, sea-blue eyes, peering from behind a skirt, with that shy, entrancing smile.

Mr Ponsonby lives alone in a red-brick farmhouse that has belonged to the Ponsonbys for generations, but he is very poor and does everything for himself. He is, therefore, a very handy man; can, in fact, turn his hand to anything.

He arrived at the cottage on foot, with a pail full of implements and packages in either hand, at the same moment as we rattled down to the middle of the lane in the old Austin Seven, and stuck there. He would cheerfully, I am sure, have lifted the Austin and ourselves across the 'splash' – a stream that crosses a moorland road – if we had wished it.

But we decided to leave Barkis where he was at the moment – Barkis is the Baby Austin, christened 'Barkis is willin'' for obvious reasons – and carry the stuff up to the cottage, for the road practically petered out where the stream crossed the track through the heather.

Now a peculiar thing about Mr Ponsonby is that, however many people there are to share a load, he always seems to attract to himself, like a magnet, not only all the heaviest and most awkward bundles, but about three times his share, even counting his size. We all know this and so we insist, on starting, that he has not more than twice what he ought to have.

He meekly starts with his load, and then about half-way you suddenly discover that Mr Ponsonby is simply lost among bundles, while some of the youngsters, perhaps, are disporting themselves care-free among the heather, or some less conscientious among the grown-ups are allowing him to be the beast of burden.

Knowing him well, I simply bully him at the start into letting everybody take her, or his, share, then I watch him with an eagle eye that dares him to take the whole of the youngsters' bundles. There were, however, no youngsters that day, so Jane and I did manage to keep him in order.

Anne Hepple
(1877 - 1959)

SCOTCH BROTH

The Old Colonel had a gardener who was typical of all gardeners, and most properly he was called Adam. Between the Colonel and himself it was sometimes difficult to tell who was the boss. I once overheard him say in the pub: 'I've got a good master. He lets I alone.' It is by this yardstick of non-intervention that gardeners judge their employers; and I heard him upbraided for his use of that old-fashioned expression, 'Master', by a smart young jackanapes who worked in a factory.

'Feudal,' said the young jackanapes, having learned the word at school. 'That's what your outlook is, Adam – feudal. Thank 'Eaven some of us 'ave grown out of that way of thinking.'

I doubt if Adam knew what 'feudal' meant, but he quelled the young man, who happened to be his nephew, with a single sentence. He said simply: 'Who be thy master, then?' And there was something in his tone which called up an endless vista of conveyor-belts and shop-stewards and foremen, anonymous managers, faceless, unknown directors, financiers, stockbrokers, banks.

The young man, knowing not whom he served nor what shareholders lived on the fruits of his labour, had nothing to say; and old Adam stalked out.

That was the only time I ever saw him ruffled; for he possessed the kind of patience which seems to be a perquisite of those who grow things and whose fortunes are bound up with the unpredictable seasons, the infinitely capricious English weather, and the slow, obstinate, inexorable forces of Nature.

Adam had the same shrug for the late frost which cut off his peaches, for the mysterious virus which shrivelled his scarlet snap-dragons just when the beds were at their best, for the summer drought and for the winter flood.

'These things,' he used to say, 'level themselves out in the end.' That phrase summarises a whole philosophy, the gardener's and the farmer's philosophy of levelling-out.

It is founded, I think, upon an assumption that the weather is shared roughly between God and the Devil, with a slight advantage on the side of God.

John Moore
(1907 – 1967)

Come Rain, Come Shine

Despite the loss of much which held country life together, some qualities remain from the old days. The most endearing is that class-conscious classlessness of the countryman. All instinctively have that essence of social awareness which is translated into English in the phrase 'knowing one's place,' and in the result no one is gauche in any company, since all are sure of where they stand. A swineherd on a duke's estate is much easier in the presence of his employer than is a machinist in that of a factory superintendent ... Both are in the service of the ancient mother goddess, Earth. They observe the same rites and share in the performance of them.

The material balance is awry, but this old ease of comradeship remains.

Thomas Firbank

(b.1910)

Log Hut

ORIGINALITY AND INDEPENDENCE

Reggie was in possession of inner warmth, and he felt in no sense inferior to anyone anywhere (but not the 'I'm-as-good-as you' attitude), nor his work of less value and importance to society than the highest in the land. He was too proud and too conscious of this; but in him even that was delightful. For one's attitude towards a man, and his own attitude towards life for that matter, depends so much upon his personality (history is governed nearly as much by this as by economic factors). Reggie had considerable personality, and of an attractive kind. Most working men look older than their arithmetical age. He looked younger. The most striking attribute of his slight wiry figure with its good-looking bronzed face, was his hair – a crop of apparently not-thinning, silky flaxen hair. Always conscious of his appearance he never wore a hat or cap – again rare amongst working men. He fitted perfectly into the woodland surroundings, as he stood leaning against a tree – he was then the best-dressed man, in his 'shabby' workman's clothes, that I have seen in the course of my life. Realising this, he frequently draped himself against a tree while gossiping in his high-pitched voice.

Taking a line each, we proceeded to underplant with beech-trees a given acreage of the thinned ash-wood. Reggie worked by fits and starts, urging the boys forward in his high voice for a period, after which he often paused for a gossip. Then some more planting followed by a further extension of gossip, this time on the characteristics of a certain foreman of the estate, who had once, but once only, attempted to interfere in the affairs of the wood, and of that man's 'ignorance' – i.e., manners – when he called at Reggie's house and looked his wife up and down. More planting, and then likely enough a brief outline of the moral life of the village owing to the influx of the military when too many girls became a soldier's relaxation. His tone on most matters was the normal one of cheerful scorn, but on this latter he was rather scandalized, for, though not in the least religious, he was very moral, and a great family man in love with his wife and daughter, proud of the way his daughter had him under her thumb and highly indignant with Beveridge for presuming to extend State Assistance towards her upkeep, for he could look after his own maid, thank you, he didn't want no state assistance for his little maid … And thus between our spurts of planting we covered a good deal of ground in conversation.

John Stewart Collis
(1900 – 1984)

THE WORM FORGIVES THE PLOUGH

Another outstanding character was Seumas. He was comparatively well educated and had a small but select library. He got two or three weekly papers and one monthly magazine – Stead's 'Review of Reviews' – and sometimes he had American and other foreign papers and periodicals sent to him from friends abroad. Seumas did not come often to the ceilidh, but when he did come mere gossip was taboo for that evening. Stories of pioneer life in Canada or Australia and political or ethical dissertations were his sort of contribution and I can yet see the eager interest of the less well-informed as they listened to his graphic discourse. Seumas was at once the best and the worst crofter in the district. He always had good crops and stock and was held in great respect by his neighbours, but accomplishments in which other men took supreme pride – for instance, a straight furrow or a well-built stack – were matters of utter indifference to him. I have seen him nearing a 'finish' in his lea ploughing with the unploughed rig yards wide at one end and run to nothing at the other, and 'a straight like a corkscrew.' When I mildly twitted him on the point he laughed unconcernedly, and told me that it was only when I mentioned the matter he realised he was ploughing; he had spent the whole forenoon just following the horses and absently turning over the ground, but his thoughts had been occupied with some poem of Burns, the run of which he had been trying to get right!

'But,' said he, 'although the furrows are crooked the oats will grow just as well as if they were straight;' and so they did, for he always used the best of seed and kept his land in a high state of fertility.

On another occasion I was giving him a hand with the leading-in of the harvest; he was building the stack and I was forking on. He kept up an interesting conversation all the time and I had to warn him repeatedly that the stack was going agee. He did try to rectify matters, but usually overdid it until, when nearly finished the stack had assumed rather a weird shape, but the builder's concern was with something in Russia. Just as the last of the standing sheaves were being fitted in at the top the whole structure came toppling to earth – with the architect half-buried in the ruins! To most stackers such a happening would have seemed a calamity but my philosophic friend merely grasped an armful of sheaves, started to build again on a new foundation, and proceeded with the tale of Siberia!

Colin MacDonald

Echoes of the Glen

Aunt Hetty was sitting in her summer-house at the water's edge, knitting a sock and keeping a look-out for them. They moored the boat at her little landing-stage and stepped ashore.

'My dears! Lovely to see you,' said Aunt Hetty, rolling up her wool and impaling the ball on her needles as though she was skewering a piece of mutton to make a shashlik. 'Come along – we're having tea in the strawberry-bed.'

'In the strawberry-bed?'

'Yes. It's a new idea that occurred to me last time Vin was here. You know how much better they always taste when you eat them straight off the plants? Only the drawback is, there's never any cream and sugar. So I thought, why not take the cream and sugar under the nets with us? We tried it, and it's a capital plan. I can't imagine why I never thought of it before.' She took Vin's arm and led the way across the lawn. The others followed, exchanging telegraphically, with a smile, their amused affection for Aunt Hetty. Glorious woman: nobody else would have had an idea like that – or rather, nobody else would have put it seriously and efficiently into practice, complete with table, chairs, silver teapot, and cucumber sandwiches. She had even had the nets heightened on poles to give more head room.

Jan Struther
(1901 – 1953)

Mrs. Miniver

SIMPLICITY AND MODESTY

The late warm light of a wintry sun had tinged with colour the white tops of the surrounding fells before Mary, listening for the peevish cry of sheep or the high note of her husband's whistle, began to be troubled by his absence. Tom knew the fells in winter and summer as he knew his own farmyard. He was not likely to be lost, but there were other perils which grew in her mind as the hours passed.

She had tended the animals and had made the round of the farm half a dozen times, partly to leave nothing for Tom to do after his wearying day, partly to keep herself occupied. Darkness came quickly after the sun dropped, and already there was a whining and a moaning in the chimney that foretold another wild night.

The first thick wet snowflakes were beginning to fill the air, laying a heavier blanket of silence on the still world of the hills when, from the slate-roofed porch of the farm, Mary saw a live black shadow moving swiftly along the rutted cartroad. It was too dark to distinguish more, but a clammy fear clutched her and she found herself breathing faster as she sensed the dog leap the wall as a short cut to the door. A moment later it was at her feet alternately nuzzling her dress, with its white-tipped tail waving like a flag, and then flopping down to pant from sheer exhaustion. Mary wasted few words as she slipped an old coat over her shoulders and a scarf round her throat.

'Good lad,' she said, 'I reckon tha's come to say he wants me.'

It was clear to her that the dog would not have come on alone if Tom had been returning. It would have been needed to keep the sheep from straying. In any case, Tom would have kept it well to heel on a night like this. Perhaps he was having difficulties in digging out the buried ewes. Maybe he couldn't find them all. Or could it be…?

She tried to banish the black visions as, with the dog close beside her, and with a flickering hurricane lamp to keep her out of the deeper snowdrifts she clambered up the steep fell track now fast becoming obliterated by the persistent fall.

When she reached the gate where the cart track led into the intake the dog ran wildly along the wall side. Twice she climbed over the gate that was already buried up to its second cross-bar, and called the animal to follow. Once it leaped on to the wall-top and barked, but it did not come to her. There was no footprint near the gate but her own, and no sound but the muffled rattle of a stream, and for a moment she felt a sudden helplessness. Then she turned to follow the dog.

She found Tom some time later at the foot of a shallow cliff, face down in the snow with one leg twisted hideously under him. Fresh snow had already begun to pile up on his back and head. His cap had fallen into a gulley and his long pole lay in two pieces projecting raggedly from a bank of snow. Mary slipped a hand into his jacket and started with faint surprise as it touched the hard shape of his tin whistle projecting from the inside pocket. He was still warm, and she could feel the slow beating of his heart.

In the dale they still tell the story of how, in a nightmare journey that lasted many hours, Mary carried him home on her back, stopping from sheer exhaustion a dozen times on the way, stumbling herself as she frequently lost the track, floundering through drifts and into icy pools, reaching home cut and bruised and limp with the weight of her burden, and of how she got him into bed and brought him back to warmth and consciousness and then set off again down the dale road to get a doctor just as the first sleepy farm hands were stirring in the half-light of dawn. It remains an outstanding epic in the land where life is often lived at epic level.

In the weeks that followed Mary nursed her Tom Boy back to health, and her own ordeal left no mark upon her. Held bedfast with a broken leg and wrist and tormented by his bruises, Tom, she declared, was easier to manage unconscious than conscious. And she laughed at the old dale doctor when he showed a desire to talk of her part in the affair.

'It were nowt at all,' she said.

Harry Scott
COUNTRYSIDE CHARACTER

But to return to Miss Matty. It was really very pleasant to see how her unselfishness and simple sense of justice called out the same good qualities in others. She never seemed to think any one would impose upon her, because she should be so grieved to do it to them. I have heard her put a stop to the asseverations of the man who brought her coals by quietly saying, 'I am sure you would be sorry to bring me wrong weight;' and if the coals were short measure that time, I don't believe they ever were again. People would have felt as much ashamed of presuming on her good faith as they would have done on that of a child. But my father says 'such simplicity might be very well in Cranford, but would never do in the world.'

Elisabeth Gaskell
(1810 - 1865)
CRANFORD

Quite subtly and without talking about it, in the few weeks since our honeymoon, May had radically changed my diet and it was having an effect. The flour she used for baking bread was less refined and the additional flavour and texture it imparted to the loaf compensated for the reduction in my butter consumption on which she insisted. It also helped to soak up the fat from the home cured bacon of which I refused to be deprived. However she gradually altered the way I ate most of that. Instead of always having it fried, I consumed more of it boiled and eaten hot with beans or cold with salad.

I thought I'd soon be bored with that. While always happy to cut up a firm and sweet tomato, crunch a crisp radish or spring onion or munch the heart of a lettuce, I'd never been a salad fanatic. But May changed all that. In preparing salads, she displayed an imagination which almost amounted to wizardry. Her principle was that nothing which was fruit or vegetable, flavoursome, fresh and wholesome need be excluded. 'The trick', she said when shrugging off any suggestion of special knowledge, 'is simple – just bite the ingredients and concentrate hard. Try to remember the flavours and that will tell you which can be mixed to provide harmony and variety.'

Her interest in preparing these dishes had been stimulated before the war when she had started to think about ways in which the diets of the world's poor could be  improved nutritionally and made more exciting. Since meat was an expensive product, and, even then, she was leaning towards vegetarian foods on compassionate grounds – eggs and dairy products provided the other major ingredients of her cuisine.

Her great joy in coming out to Shropshire, she told me, was to be able to obtain so easily supplies of rich, full cream milk which hadn't been pasteurised.

'A miraculous living medium,' she called it, 'in which the bacteria it contains can be managed just like a crop. Encouraged to develop or remain quiescent by merely changing the temperature or conditions under which the milk is kept. It's a system which can also be used to multiply other organisms which will process it for you as they grow.'

As I stood stamping to warm my feet and peeping eastwards in the hope of glimpsing the first freckle of welcome light, I chuckled. I was remembering how quickly May had won over my mother to her ways of thinking. We'd always deliberately soured milk at Fordhall and then strained the curds through muslin to produce cheese as a change from our Farmhouse Cheshire or the rarer Blue Cheshires which Mother made. But May amazed her by the variety of cream cheeses she prepared. Apart from the inclusion of chopped, fresh cucumber or chives which were old country standbys, Mother considered May's inclusions exciting and audacious. Other herbs like mint, thyme or chervil were commonplaces. But chopped celery, grated apple, shredded pineapple, chopped walnuts, raisins, thinly sliced green peppers from a friend's Birmingham glass-house or rare powdered red paprika from a continental warehouse in Shrewsbury all joyfully assailed our unsophisticated palates. As one exciting recipe followed another, Mother's admiration for May's talent became almost embarrassing. Repeatedly, when we were alone, she'd clutch my hand and squeeze it conspiratorially and murmur 'That's a wonderful girl that you have married.'

Arthur Hollins
(b.1915)
THE FARMER, THE PLOUGH AND THE DEVIL

HAPPINESS AND JOY

Most of the men sang or whistled as they dug or hoed. There was a good deal of outdoor singing in those days. Workmen sang at their jobs; men with horses and carts sang on the road; the baker, the miller's man, and the fish-hawker sang as they went from door to door; even the doctor and the parson on their rounds hummed a tune between their teeth. People were poorer and had not the comforts, amusements, or knowledge we have to day; but they were happier. Which seems to suggest that happiness depends more upon the state of mind – and body, perhaps – than upon circumstances and events.

Flora Thompson
(1876 – 1947)

LARK RISE TO CANDLEFORD

David was born in 1717 in the isolated village of Imber, in the middle of Salisbury Plain (now derelict, being in the middle of a military training ground). As a youth he used to walk over to Seend in the evenings after work, to attend chapel meeting – a journey of seven or eight miles each way. Then he married and for more than thirty years was employed, upon one farm, as a shepherd. 'He conversed daily with his Bible and always found matter there for his thoughts; while every object in the field, the sheep, the pasture, the sky and his own occupation, all brought to mind a psalm, a prophecy, a parable or some other blessed portion of the Scriptures'.

He and his wife had sixteen children, in such rapid succession that there were twelve of them around the table at once. A Dr Stonehouse who visited them paints a frightening picture of the austerity of their lives. David earned a wage of 6s 3d a week, out of which he sometimes had to pay an assistant. His cottage had one room downstairs and one upstairs. Evidently there were no cupboards or shelves for he had to keep his big Bible up under the thatch. They seldom had a fire, and rain came through the thatch to beat on their bed. The little girls went gathering stray wisps of wool, which they washed, carded, spun and used for knitting stockings. The little boys went bird scaring and picking stones. The mother suffered from rheumatism, through starting work too soon after the birth of one of her children. They regarded water-gruel, flavoured with ale and honey, as a great luxury.

Yet he seems to have been truly happy and contented. Said he, 'My great Master had every state and condition of life at His choice, and chose a hard one, while I only submit to the lot that is appointed to me.' Incidentally, he lived to be eighty and died in his sleep.

Ralph Whitlock
(1914 – 1995)

A FAMILY AND A VILLAGE

To every cot the lord's indulgent mind
Has a small space for garden-ground assign'd;
Here – till return of morn dismiss'd the farm
The careful peasant plies the sinewy arm,
Warm'd as he works, and casts his look around
On every foot of that improving ground:
It is his own he sees; his master's eye
Peers not about, some secret fault to spy;
Nor voice severe is there, nor censure known;
Hope, profit, pleasure, – they are all his own.
Here grow the humble cives, and, hard by them,
The leek with crown globose and reedy stem;
High climb his pulse in many an even row,
Deep strike the ponderous roots in soil below;
And herbs of potent smell and pungent taste
Give a warm relish to the night's repast.
Apples and cherries grafted by his hand,
And cluster'd nuts for neighbouring market stand.
Nor thus concludes his labour; near the cot,
The reed fence rises round some fav'rite spot;
Where rich carnations, pinks with purple eyes,
Proud hyacinths, the least some florist's prize,
Tulips tall-stemmed and pounced auriculas rise.
   Here on Sunday-eve, when service ends,
Meet and rejoice a family of friends;
All speak aloud, are happy and are free,
And glad they seem, and gaily they agree.
   What, though fastidious ears may shun the speech,
Where all are talkers and where none can teach;
Where still the welcome and the words are old,
And the same stories are for ever told;
Yet theirs is joy that, bursting from the heart,
Prompts the glad tongue these nothings to impart;
That forms these tones of gladness we despise,

That lifts their steps, that sparkles in their eyes;
That talks or laughs or runs or shouts or plays,
And speaks in all their looks and all their ways.

George Crabbe
(1754 - 1832)
from *The Parish Register,* Part 1, Baptisms

Dr. Hemming dresses by candlelight and goes stamping downstairs. Mrs Hemming, in spite of his protests, follows him and hands him his black leather bag. As she returns to her cold bed, she can hear the roar of the starting engine and a grating of gears (Dr Hemming is not a good driver) and the whine of the worn transmission as it dies away in the distance.

Dr Hemming sits in the car, encouraging the tremulous young husband: he knows what it feels like, he says, when your wife has her first. He is now wide awake and aware, once again, of the strange exhilaration that comes to a man when, roused from slumber, he finds himself suddenly transported and whirled into the emptiness and silence of the nocturnal earth. He has often before seen Monk's Norton and the woods and the great rolling claylands transfigured by sleep; yet each time that he sees them – in spring when the headlights' beam reveals plum-blossom flecking bare orchards like flurried snow, in mid-summer nights when the sky never loses all light, when hedgerows are pallid with billowing clouds of elderbloom and gauzy ghost-moths eddy in the beam like wind-blown petals; in autumn, when mist lies in vagrant patches, like fog at sea, and earth is trackless as sky; on November nights when stars glitter like powdered crystal, and meteors, unseen by other men's eyes, slide silently over the vault and flare and are gone – in all these rare manifestations of beauty he is made aware of the earth's solemn magnitude and of a mystery in which his own insignificance and that of all the transient human life which he tends are the strangest part.

These ecstatic, unreasoned, sudden perceptions of awe and
of beauty are, perhaps, Dr Hemming's nearest approaches to a
mystical or a religious mood. He is not, in the ordinary
acceptance of the term (the Rector's, for example), a religious
man. He is too nearly concerned with the defects and the
weaknesses of men's mortal bodies and with the obvious
emergencies of existence, such as birth and death, to trouble
himself much about their immortal souls. Yet not even the most
captious or cynical of his neighbours can deny that, according
to his lights (which are those of broad day: these nocturnal
exaltations being, in his case, a lapse from the normal), he is a
good man; the better perhaps because, in spite of the pitiful
degradations of human flesh and spirit with which, on occasion,
his practice confronts him, he has a natural inclination to see
good in his fellow men. If he is not particularly gifted or skilful
– and he doesn't pretend to be either – he is kind and honest
and wise and courageous and merciful. Whatever the next world
may hold in store for him, he has his reward in this: it would be
difficult in Monk's Norton (or all England) to find a more
happy man.

Francis Brett Young
(1884 – 1954)
Portrait of a Village

AWARENESS OF GOD

So down he sat, and at his companion's suggestion lit his
pipe. This, thought James, was true enjoyment. He gave himself
up to it, wondering what Alice would say if she saw him, and
deciding boldly that he didn't think he cared much. And they
began to talk – at first in their ordinary voices, but soon dropping
into undertones because of the beauty, the immense, absorbed,

hushed beauty of the night, with the moon a day past its full, beginning to sail over the top of Burdon Down behind them, and part the apple-leaves with silver fingers. And presently they didn't even talk, but sat quite still, just as if for years they had been easy friends, and together they watched the great yew-tree on the other side of the little sleeping garden brushing its dark and solemn head across the stars, and listened to the cry of an owl, floating from somewhere very far away towards them on the silence.

To Jen, who had hardly known what silence was, it was a revelation. She listened, dissolved in a kind of awestruck joy. It seemed to her as if she were in the presence of perfect holiness, as if she were close to the very feet of God. She who had been trained irreligiously became, in this beauty, religious. She wanted to worship and fall down; she wanted to praise the Lord her Maker. And forgetting James, who anyhow was very easily forgotten, under her breath she murmured 'And the Glory of the Lord was revealed' – for father had seen to it that she studied the Bible carefully, it being, he assured her, English literature at its best.

James' heart gave a thump. That she should say what he so often said to himself on similar occasions struck him as very wonderful.

FATHER
by the Author of ELIZABETH AND HER GERMAN GARDEN

The ledge was an enchanted place. Here one fine day this summer Ignatius had sat for seven hours, absorbed, watching the play of light on sea and land, seven hours that passed as one. The wind altered every few minutes, the sun wheeled across from Ignatius's left shoulder to his right, the preoccupied sea changed its mind and wandered; then by degrees all accustomed images of thought left him, there were neither words nor metaphors, sea and earth existed on their own terms, and he was gradually absorbed into all he saw, till he lost human consciousness, and became one of many objects, a part of the coast, drained of his identity, persisting mindless like a patch of obstinate sunlight gleaming on the water a mile from shore, a patch of which he was without thought aware, just as without thought he was aware of himself sitting on the ledge: dimly, from time to time aware, but without distinction between his body pressing upon the rock or the rock pressing up against his body: human consciousness passed out from him, yet not into sleep; into no blurring of sense, though into something stiller than human sense: something clear and shining, wind touched, shadow crossed; something at once firm and rooted like the sun-warmed rock, cool and flowing like the water, outspread like the pine branches, high as the clouds, volatile as the air – something with perceptions extended in all these, something infinitesimal yet supreme, fragment and whole, wave, beam of light, path that the gull had not yet taken through the air: something which, when the elated mind tried to realise it, broke up thus into a thousand facets, but which in spells of deepest experience sank to a luminous sense of peace; light and water and stillness in a pool as wide as the sky. It was an experience not to be put into words, for the effort to find words at once split up the central unity of awareness into a series of particular visions; creating multiplicity; shattering a timeless exaltation into restlessness, breaking eternity into succession and the intervals between one object and another. Just as when, three parts asleep, one can at will remember the position of one's limbs, and then relax to a tide of dream, so Ignatius could in multiplicity remember himself and divide the place into units, or empty himself and be one with the scene of which he was a part. Life, or spirit, call it what one would, was manifested variously in living things and in trees and air and stones. Ignatius for a while had seen the barrier broken down, relapsing through his special identity to the principle which he expressed, which all this coast expressed, affirming his union with it and its union with him; regressing from the details imposed by time to a truth outside it. When he came to himself, his limbs stiff and numb, his mind was so charged with luminous wisdom and tranquillity that for a few moments he knew that there was no human problem he could not solve, and that, by the light which was slowly fading within his mind, he could illumine his own life and the lives of others. But the light faded; the great satisfying chord hummed away over the far horizon, and there remained only the faint piping notes of petty detail, the straying, unresolved motifs and burdens of the Symphony.

L.A.G. Strong
(1898 – 1958)

CORPORAL TUNE

It was once my lot to visit frequently an old woman of eighty, who might be not unfairly described as a mystic, or at least as possessing the mystical temperament in a high degree. She might have struck those meeting her for the first time as being rather dour and grim, but as one heard the recital of her life history one could only wonder that so much humanity and neighbourliness had survived in her. Her life had been for the most part a fight with literal starvation. Her husband had been a brute who drank and ill-treated her, and then had died leaving her with many little children. These she had somehow brought up by hook or by crook; struggling, fighting, following, finding any honest means of turning a penny. She had insisted on church, and as far as possible on school for all of them, and had herself been all her life not only a regular worshipper, but a communicant. She held, and what among the poor is exceedingly unusual, she intelligently expressed in conversation, a doctrine that was definitely sacramental, but she looked upon this life-long habitual religion merely as an outer court, as something preparatory to an illumination which she believed she had received late in life. She had no doubt whatever of the objective reality of this experience. She had fallen one day, not asleep, but into a sort of trance. She found herself going on a journey on foot, to use her own language, 'going thro' fields where there were a lot of women working in bright-coloured clothes,' and she had gone on and on till she came into the Presence of Our Lord. As I remember her narration, I do not think any words were spoken, but there was some sort of silent communication, as a result of which all fear and all uncertainty had left her for ever. 'I'm a sinner, I know,' she said, 'but since then I've never been a miserable sinner.' She did not appear to think that to pass through such an experience was necessary, and in no way despised those who had not had it, nor did she consider herself as their superior. 'It's a thing that generally comes to older people, I think,' she would say, 'to them that's getting on in life.' She seemed to think, however, that something like it would at some time be granted to every really faithful soul.

R.L. Gales
(1862 - 1927)

Vanished Country Folk

That same year, as though to balance the setback of the pigs, we received a tremendous boost on the land. As usual we had planted a potato crop and were now preparing to harvest. A surveyor from the Potato Marketing Board, to whom we were selling the crop, had visited us earlier in the season to measure up and tell us how many tons of potatoes we could expect. His figure was 45 tons. Out of that he reckoned we would have three tons of 'brock' – tiny potatoes that would be riddled out during the packing process – and so our total expected sale would be 42 tons.

I was happy with that because I had extra bills to pay that month and the money would go a long way towards meeting them. So it was with some satisfaction that we began packing the potatoes the following Monday. The Board had asked us to bag up ten tons per day, which was a reasonable output for three men working together, and so we brought up the sorting machine to the potato heap and set to.

By late afternoon every trace of the morning's smile had been wiped away. We had bagged up ten tons of ware and it looked as though we'd got a good third of the pile.

Despondent, I sent up a silent prayer. 'Oh Lord, there's not going to be forty-two tons of potatoes here. There's not even going to be thirty!'

I don't know whether the men had realised this, but they certainly took notice the following day when, strangely, the situation was reversed.

'I dunno,' said one, as we completed another ten tons, 'this pile don't seem to be gettin' any smaller.'

Which was true because we hadn't moved the sorter any further into the potato heap all day. And we didn't move it for the rest of the day, either. In fact that machine stayed where it was throughout Tuesday and Wednesday.

By the end of that third day, having now bagged 30 tons, we were all amazed. All, that is, except the man from the Potato Marketing Board. He was just puzzled. He'd come down to see how we were getting on and decided there was definitely something very odd going on. This man was dealing with potato mountains all the time and he knew his business.

'You're not bringing in potatoes from somewhere else, are you?' he asked. He'd now taken delivery of 30 tons of potatoes and we hadn't yet got half the pile!

'Certainly not,' I said. 'We've only got the one heap.'

The following day he was back with his chief to measure the field again and when they came into the barn they were both shaking their heads.

'It's not possible,' said the surveyor. 'You're sure you're not bringing in potatoes from somewhere else?'

By now I couldn't resist a smile. 'I'm sure, and the men here will bear me out.'

He shook his head again and glanced at the potato heap. 'Doesn't make sense,' he muttered. 'You're getting more potatoes out of the heap than it is possible to get.'

Jim Wilkinson
(b.1930)

MIRACLE VALLEY

INDEX OF AUTHORS

We have been unable to trace the name of the Author of ELIZABETH AND HER GERMAN GARDEN from whose FATHER we have used an extract (p.260).